THE NATIONAL INSTITUTE OF
ECONOMIC AND SOCIAL RESEARCH

Occasional Papers
XXXVI

THE DIFFUSION OF
MATURE TECHNOLOGIES

THE NATIONAL INSTITUTE OF ECONOMIC AND
SOCIAL RESEARCH

OFFICERS OF THE INSTITUTE

2 DEAN TRENCH STREET, SMITH SQUARE, LONDON, SWIP 3HE
The National Institute of Economic and Social Research is an independent, non-profit-making body, founded in 1938. It has as its aim the promotion of realistic research, particularly in the field of economics. It conducts research by its own research staff and in cooperation with the universities and other academic bodies. The results of the work done under the Institute's auspices are published in several series, and a list of its recent publications will be found at the end of this volume.

THE DIFFUSION OF MATURE TECHNOLOGIES

GEORGE F. RAY

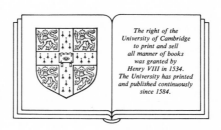

The right of the
University of Cambridge
to print and sell
all manner of books
was granted by
Henry VIII in 1534.
The University has printed
and published continuously
since 1584.

CAMBRIDGE UNIVERSITY PRESS

CAMBRIDGE

LONDON   NEW YORK   NEW ROCHELLE
MELBOURNE   SYDNEY

Published by the Press Syndicate of the University of Cambridge
The Pitt Building, Trumpington Street, Cambridge CB2 1RP
32 East 57th Street, New York, NY 10022, USA
296 Beaconsfield Parade, Middle Park, Melbourne 3206, Australia

First published 1984

Printed in Great Britain at the University Press, Cambridge

Library of Congress catalogue card number: 83-14467

British Library Cataloguing in Publication Data
Ray, George
The diffusion of mature technologies.—(National
Institute of Economic and Social Research.
Occasional papers; 36)
1. Industry   2. Technological innovations
I. Title   II. Series
338'.06   HC79.I4
ISBN 0 521 26008 6

CONTENTS

TABLES

SYMBOLS IN THE TABLES

. . . not available
— nil or negligible
n.a. not applicable

CHARTS

Tables

ACKNOWLEDGEMENTS

We are most grateful for the assistance received for this project from the Anglo-German Foundation for the Study of Industrial Society.

This project was undertaken jointly by the National Institute of Economic and Social Research in London and the Ifo-Institut für Wirtschaftsforschung in Munich. Mr L. Uhlmann, from the Ifo-Institut, conducted the inquiry covering Germany, as well as a good deal of the research into technical and trade literature. In Sweden, the Industriens Utredningsinstitut, represented by Mr J. Örtengren, participated in the project, in France Mrs Casanova-Mazière from the Bureau d'Informations et de Prévisions Economiques and in Italy, Mr I. Cipoletta, from the Istituto Nazionale per lo Studio della Congiuntura. Their contribution to the project was invaluable. (In the text these institutes are referred to by their abbreviations, that is, IFO, IUI, BIPE and ISCO.)

Many other organisations and experts helped with advice and information and thanks are also due to them for their willing assistance.

ABBREVIATIONS

Because the names of the technologies studied occur so frequently we have shortened them in the text as follows:
basic oxygen steelmaking – BOP
continuous casting – CC
tunnel kilns in brickmaking – TK
shuttleless looms – SL
float glass – FG
numerically controlled machine tools – NCMT.

INTRODUCTION

The National Institute published a study on the diffusion of *new* industrial processes in 1974.[1] The purpose of that book was to study the introduction and diffusion of major postwar process innovations in several industrial countries, to analyse the factors which facilitated or hindered the adoption of new techniques in industry, the time pattern of their diffusion and the influences to which they were subject.

Eight major processes were selected and their diffusion measured and analysed in the same way in Austria, Italy, Sweden, the United Kingdom, the United States and West Germany, thus permitting an international comparison of the results. The book was the outcome of international teamwork.

A very brief summary of the main findings of the original work will provide a background for this book. First, it established that there were considerable international differences in the diffusion of the selected new processes. On average, the greatest spread of diffusion has been achieved in Sweden, with the United Kingdom second and the same two countries, in reverse order, led in terms of the date of the first introduction. Germany and Austria, however, tended to be the quickest to reach a substantial measure of diffusion, that is, the deepest penetration of the new technologies. These results led us to suggest very cautiously that, in countries which had been pioneers, diffusion had tended to be slower.

Three factors which appeared to have had the most significant and general influences were, firstly, the advantage given by the new process in terms of overall profitability; secondly, the attitude of management to the adoption of new techniques; and thirdly, access to capital. Profitability seemed to contribute to the explanation of the different speeds of diffusion, particularly when relative factor prices played a significant part. Introducing the new process very often increased the capacity of the firm, hence the potential market was also important in the profitability calculations and, consequently, in the speed of diffusion. To some extent, institutional differences also helped to explain different levels and speeds of diffusion, as did the varying structure of industry. There was some evidence that certain firms tended to be early or late in the introduction of all new processes, not just the one under review. The possibility that the profitability calculations were intertwined with management attitudes was examined and (as the unexplained residuals were still quite large) it was concluded that management attitudes probably were an important factor, albeit unquantifiable.

No country had an outstanding general lead in introducing new techniques and a number of reasons were found for the differences among countries. Differences in wage levels were most important in some cases, different rates of growth of consumption in others, and different plant structures in yet other instances.

THE SCOPE OF THE PRESENT STUDY

The analysis in the first book was based on the situation at the end of the 1960s. More than twelve years have now passed and the processes which were then relatively new have matured. The aim of the present study is to follow up the same processes in order to analyse their diffusion after the initial period of introduction. The original study of the international team covered eight major new processes. The present analysis extends to six of them: basic oxygen steelmaking, continuous casting of steel, numerically controlled machine tools, float glass, tunnel kilns in brickmaking and shuttleless looms. We have dropped two processes which were originally included (special presses in papermaking and gibberellic acid in malting) on the grounds that they are probably less important than the others.

Our new study differs from the earlier one in some other respects too. The first difference is in the international coverage. It was our intention from the outset to concentrate on Germany and the United Kingdom but we decided that wider international experience might help to put the situation in these two countries into perspective. The study has, therefore, been extended in two directions. Wherever international information has made it possible, additional countries have been included, extra to those covered by our original report. Moreover, with the help of economic research institutes abroad, we have collected information beyond mere statistics. In addition to that from Germany and the United Kingdom, such information has been available from Italy, Sweden and also – a new-comer to this project – France. The information received from institutes in these countries has provided a valuable supplement to the main body of research conducted by the National Institute in London and the Ifo-Institut für Wirtschaftsforschung in Munich.

The second main difference concerns the method we used to collect information. Instead of large-scale postal and personal inquiries, which were very difficult and time consuming in the earlier study, we obtained most of the necessary statistical information from central national and international sources.

There is, however, an obvious problem here. The overall diffusion of any innovation within an industry conceals the specific situation of the individual enterprises. This may vary considerably so that the adoption of a major innovation in one company and its rejection in another firm in the same industry may be rationally justified. There is the additional possibility of different attitudes among managements which may also be concealed by the average. Ideally, our investigation of each process ought to cover each company likely to be a potential candidate for the adoption. Such a procedure was beyond our resources. However, in order to close this gap, at least partially, we contacted a small number of major companies, as well as organisations that could be supposed to act as spokesmen for their particular industry, in order to find out more about the processes studied and, where applicable, their reasons for the rejection or late adoption of the technology in question. The picture which emerges will not be complete, for precisely the reason mentioned; nevertheless, we believe that an average picture, with the additional information collected in a number of countries, will convey the position of the industry as a whole and of the extent of its willingness to innovate.

A new dimension has also been added to the original study. The innovations in question were relatively new at the time of our first inquiry and might have been further improved or even replaced by newer processes. Similarly, the earlier technology might have fought its way back to regain its former share of its own particular market. These aspects of the situation, both of which we cover in this study, were obviously impossible to investigate at the time of the first inquiry since they require a historical perspective.

To sum up then, for each of the six technological processes presently under review we wanted to collect information on the following points.

1. Some measure of the diffusion of the technology; it was obvious from the outset that this was dependent on the statistics available and might therefore vary from process to process.
2. The technical (or other) development of the process since the late 1960s.
3. The reasons for either rapid or slow diffusion and, in the case of the latter, an explanation for the survival of the earlier technology.
4. The requirements of products or sections of production that are unsuited to the new technology.
5. Any specific factors promoting or hindering further adoption.
6. Whether there is room for further development of the process or whether it will be replaced in the foreseeable future by some even newer technology.
7. Whether size (of the plant or the company) has any effect on the adoption of the process.

8. The effect of higher energy prices on the technology.
9. Finally, various specialist questions were asked which are relevant only to particular cases.

The extent to which these questions could be answered varied from process to process. Each of the six major technologies is discussed in a separate chapter. Similar chapters in the earlier study described the technology of the processes at length. This time the technical details will be confined to those needed to illustrate the development of the technology since the late 1960s and some particular aspect may, perhaps, also be studied.

OXYGEN STEELMAKING

The basic oxygen process (BOP) in steelmaking has been of historic importance. By the end of the 1960s, over 70 per cent of Japanese steel was made using this process, which was then relatively new, whilst only two of the minor producers (Austria, which pioneered it, and the Netherlands) had reached a comparable degree of diffusion. In the United States, Germany and Belgium the process was in use for only 40 per cent of steel production and considerably less in the other European producing countries.[1] BOP has since spread remarkably rapidly. In many advanced steelmaking countries its dissemination has probably reached or even surpassed its peak, so that it is now possible to have some idea of its historical significance.

Chart 2.1 traces the changes in steelmaking processes by indicating their importance in the United States steel industry, the largest in the West, in the past 120 years. Fundamentally new and superior processes were generally rapidly adopted. Within ten to fifteen years the Bessemer process replaced crucible steel and at its peak the open hearth process was introduced but it took much longer, thirty to forty years, before reaching Bessemer's earlier importance. BOP's ascent has been more rapid, taking only fifteen years, but instead of the earlier peaks of over 80 per cent of all steel production reached by the Bessemer and open hearth processes, it probably reached its limit at just above 60 per cent. (The United States steel industry has been lagging in both the introduction and the diffusion of BOP; the reasons for this have been analysed in great detail by Rosegger.)[2]

Open hearth production still accounted for 11 per cent of United States steel in 1981, the highest share, apart from Canada, among major Western producers. This process is likely to be eliminated soon but part of it will probably be replaced by electric steel rather than BOP. The share of electric steel rose from small beginnings more than half a century ago to over one quarter by 1980. More modern types of electric steelmaking have given a new lease of life to this old-established process and it has been expanding rapidly, competing with BOP to replace the open hearth in the United States and elsewhere.

The development of steelmaking processes follows broadly similar lines in the other major producing countries. Some countries preferred the Thomas process (which considerably modified the Bessemer principle in

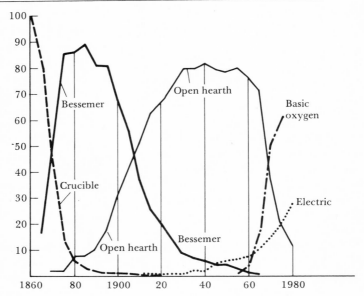

Source: Historical statistics of the US.

Chart 2.1 *United States steel production, by technologies, 1860–1979, per cent share in total output*

order to use ores with a high phosphorus content) and, in those countries, it survived much longer than Bessemer had elsewhere. Around 1970 it was still the leading process in countries such as France and Belgium (much more important locally than the open hearth) because of the specific qualities of domestic ores. In other countries the upswing of BOP's time path started earlier than in the United States, for example in Japan, where new steelworks adopted the newest technology almost automatically. In some countries electric steel became important much earlier than elsewhere, as in Scandinavia, where cheap hydropower gave the process an advantage. Overall, the replacement of the earlier process by a combination of BOP and electric steel has been universal.

The result, common to all the changes in steelmaking in the past thirty years, has been the speed-up of productive operations and an increase in the scale of output in order to reduce unit costs. BOP has been the main vehicle of these trends. Apart from its inherent advantages of a large reduction in production time and lower costs generally, and of a reduction in energy requirements in particular, BOP has drastically raised the minimum efficient scale of integrated steel plant and also altered the basic material needs of large bulk steelmaking; oxygen converters operate with hot metal making up 70–75 per cent or more of the charge.

This latter factor had other important implications. It meant that there was no more than 30 per cent of scrap in the charge, compared with an average of about 50 per cent of scrap fed into open hearth production which is more flexible in this respect. This change in the composition of the charge contributed to the economic viability of electric steelmaking, which uses 90 per cent or more scrap as basic material. It also promoted the spread of mini-mills which, without exception, operate electric arc furnaces. The availability of scrap has always been crucial to electric steelmaking, whose economy is to a large extent dependent on its price. The spread of BOP reduced the use of scrap in the large integrated works and thus made more available for the electric steelmakers who were generally operating on a smaller scale. The reduced demand for scrap from the large producers also led to lower prices and thus made electric steel more profitable.

BOP, therefore, has had a dual influence on the economies of scale of steelmaking: upwards, by raising the minimum efficient scale of the large, integrated plants and downwards, by widening the scope for the more efficient operation of smaller steel plant. This second effect has resulted in the increase of mini-plants, whose technology has been further helped by another major innovation, continuous casting, which we discuss in the next chapter.[3] In addition, since the specific primary energy requirements of electric arc furnace steelmaking with 100 per cent scrap charge are the lowest of all steelmaking processes, no energy being necessary for the reduction of ore (iron oxide) to iron, the post-1973 energy situation was an additional factor in favour of electric steel.

RECENT DEVELOPMENTS IN THE STEELMAKING PROCESS

The first commercial application of BOP in the early 1950s took the form of the LD-converter (so-called after the first two Austrian works that built it: Linz and Donawitz). By the late 1950s and particularly in the 1960s, the original technology had been further developed in various directions. The converter size was enlarged and its capacity raised by various other new developments in order to increase output, for example, by increasing the speed of rotation of the converter. The original LD had introduced oxygen from the top of the converter; now lances injected it from the bottom and/or side of the converter, aiming at better oxidation as well as allowing the processing of iron with high phosphorus content (impossible in the original version). Powdered lime was mixed into the oxygen stream also to allow the use of high-phosphorus ores and this was called the LD-AC or OLP process. There were other changes also. Some of these developments permitted a somewhat higher proportion in the charge of scrap than was possible in the earlier versions of the oxygen furnace.

The further advance during and after the 1970s followed partly the same objectives: those of increasing the scrap ratio, of improving quality by combining top and bottom blowing of the oxygen stream and experimenting with bottom blowing alone, of adding inert gases (Ar or N_2, that is argon or nitrogen) to the oxygen flow and of reducing tapping time. New objectives have also arisen, such as reducing pollution of the steelworks in general and, as a result of the changed energy situation which dramatically raised costs in this energy-hungry industry, more attention has had to be paid to the use and cost of all types of fuel. Considerable advances in instrumentation, measurement and control have helped to approach these objectives.

In the course of research and development a fair number of variations on the original LD system have been introduced and most of them put into practice to varying degrees.[4] One of them, OBM, which was probably inspired by the AOD process in stainless steel production, was applied to the old Thomas converter and consists of injecting oxygen into Thomas converters from the bottom. It was of particular importance in France and Belgium, where about half the crude steel output in the late 1960s was produced by the Thomas process and to a lesser extent in Germany, where this proportion was about 15 per cent at the same time. This conversion has resulted in higher quality steel, a reduction in energy usage and less pollution of the steelworks environment. However, such a conversion is only a temporary solution since the size of the Thomas-cum-OBM converter is usually a fraction of the modern LD converter and therefore unlikely to remain competitive in bulk steel production.

The tapping time of BOP converters (including all the various newer types) has been gradually reduced to between 30 and 45 minutes; the small OBM converters operate even faster. This compares with eight to ten hours at the open hearth. Moreover, the investment costs of BOP are lower, however calculated, than those of an open hearth plant. Another aspect that has gained great importance since 1973 is that of energy input and its cost; there are several reports on the very marked advantage of BOP over the open hearth in this area (among them, see Meyer and Herregat *op. cit.*), indicating, crudely, a halving of energy costs. Basically, the oxygen process is by its nature exothermic, that is, it emits heat; in fact, one of the roles of the scrap to be added to charge is to reduce temperature. Of course, energy is needed to produce the high quality oxygen.

Among the important advances in the area of the control of the steelmaking process, some should be mentioned here: the instrumental analysis of waste gases; the measuring of the sound generated when oxygen is blown into the converter to determine the thickness of the slag; the use of secondary lances to measure both the temperature of the steel and its carbon content; and the weighing of the vessel. All are aimed at controlling the process in order to improve steel quality and in particular to determine when the steel is ready for tapping. The development of instrumentation in general and of electronics in particular has helped to extend, by these and other minor innovations or modifications, the possibilities of controlling the process on a more scientific basis.

These developments have resulted not only in the further reduction of production costs, but also in the extension of the technical capability of BOP. Now almost all steel varieties, with few exceptions, can be produced by BOP. The permitted P-content has been very greatly reduced and the scrap ratio increased, albeit only moderately. For example, in Germany, the largest producer in Western Europe, it is indicated that the share of special steels (high carbon, alloy, and so on) in oxygen steel increased from 6 per cent in 1970 to 16 per cent in 1981. This raised the share of BOP in all special steel production from 23 per cent to 59 per cent in that period, and refuted the view still current in the second half of the 1960s that BOP was not applicable, or at least not well suited, to the production of special steels. This is not to deny that the majority of special steels, especially in some countries, is still made in electric furnaces and likely to remain so.

The average capacity of the BOP converters just about doubled during the 1970s. This is only partly the result of technical advance, since vessel sizes generally have not exceeded about 350 tonnes each, with two operating at any given time. The rise in the average size is rather the result of the phasing out of older, smaller converters and sometimes their replacement by larger ones, as well as of the increasing productivity of the remaining plants. Changes in Germany and Sweden, the largest European makers of, respectively, steel and special steel, will suffice to demonstrate this particular point.

As table 2.1 indicates, the increased capacity per plant was not a unique characteristic of BOP. The average capacity of electric furnaces has also risen and the same can be said of the few remaining German open hearths.[5] No doubt the recession in the steel industry towards the end of the 1970s contributed to this, forcing many smaller producers out of business, as well as closing the smaller plants of larger producers.

Technological advance has not been restricted to BOP, however. Electric steelmaking, its remaining major competitor or perhaps rather partner in production, has also experienced considerable progress and change. The advances in measuring and control and the allied instrumentation have made themselves felt in electric steelmaking too. The electric method offers particular advantages in cases where the volume of the production programme does not reach the minimum size of the economic operations of oxygen converters; hence it is the basic production system for the mushrooming mini-steelworks. Various technological innovations in mini-steelworks are described in *Mini-mill monographs (op.cit)* and an idea of

Table 2.1 *Average capacity of steel plants, thousand tons per year*

		BOP converters	Electric furnaces	Open hearth
Germany:	1970	698	28	121
	1975	916	42	151
	1980	1,115	73	186
Sweden:	1975	327	26	. .
	1980	454	41	. .
	1981	620	43	. .

Source: IFO and IUI calculations based on national statistics.

their proliferation can be given just by looking at the numbers listed there for the various countries (see table 2.2). Mini-works often produce steel for local requirements and it is therefore not surprising that in newly industrialising countries (for example, Brazil, Taiwan, Korea) the number of mini-plants is large. It is more noteworthy that the number is even larger in some of the advanced steelmaking countries, such as the United States and Japan (see table 2.2). This indicates the considerable penetration of small steelworks and, almost by definition, of electric steelmaking, into the markets of integrated large plants.

The list on which table 2.2 is based should be regarded with some caution. First, it is unlikely to be complete and secondly, its definition of mini-plants is somewhat obscure, reflected in the capacity figures given for each company, ranging from 30,000 tonnes to over one million tonnes (possibly in several plants) in a few cases. The flexibility of the mini-plant concept is, however, considerable. As the introduction to the journal cited mentions, some of these plants are fully integrated with their direct-reduction plants; some (at least one) include a strip mill; some produce bars, others rolled sections, wire rods or special quality products.

The direct reduction of iron (DRI), a method now in use in some of these mini-mills, is another technology used in making iron, the base material of steel. The principle of this technology has been known for thousands of years. It was revived about thirty years ago but it is only in the last ten years that it has been accepted as a route to ironmaking. In this process, pellets of iron ore are reduced in a kiln, generally by using reformed natural gas, although processes using coal instead of natural gas are also being developed. Its advantages as compared with the traditional blast furnace are significant: much smaller scale and also, even relatively, much smaller initial capital costs, no need for coke at all, easier control (it can be switched on and off safely) and simpler maintenance. Because of these advantages and in particular because of the smaller size, it seems ideal for providing

Table 2.2. *Mini-steelworks*[a]

	Number	Average capacity[b]		Number	Average capacity[b]
Western Europe			*Other industrial countries* (cont)		
Austria	2	82	New Zealand	2	133
Finland	1	240	South Africa	5	248
France	3	170	US	50	309
Germany	6	512			
Greece	4	262	*Industrialising countries*		
Ireland	1	. .	Argentina	5	152
Italy	62	. .	Brazil	14	169
Norway	1	190	Hong Kong	2	105
Portugal	1	200	South Korea	6	628
Spain	25	. .	Mexico	14	200
Sweden	1	280	Singapore	1	400
Switzerland	3	. .	Taiwan	18	71
Turkey	3	. .	Venezuela	3	260
UK	7	367			
Yugoslavia	1	. .	*Developing countries*[c]		
			Colombia	4	58
Other industrial countries			India	7	71
Canada	7	388	Indonesia	7	70
Israel	1	250	Malaysia	4	68
Japan	64	350	Philippines	7	75
			Thailand	5	119

[a]As listed in *Mini-mill monographs*, supplement to *Metal Bulletin Monthly*, December 1981.
[b]Thousand tons crude steel.
[c]Apart from those listed, one mini-mill in each of the following: Angola (30), Costa Rica (40), Dominican Republic (65), Dubai (36), Egypt (70), Ghana (35), Iran, Iraq (400), Jordan, Lebanon, Puerto Rico (120), Qatar (400), El Salvador (100), Syria, Trinidad (500) and Zaire. Figures in brackets indicate capacity, where available.)

iron for smaller steelworks. Nevertheless, there are certain problems associated with DRI, most importantly that the solid sponge iron which it produces can be used as solid charge like scrap in practically unlimited quantities in electric arc furnaces, but not in converters which rely on molten iron, although there too it can be added to scrap.[6] DRI technology probably remains in its infancy, however, since despite these theoretical advantages DRI capacity in the whole world is estimated at only about 20 million tonnes in 1981.[7]

THE DIFFUSION OF BOP

The pioneering period for BOP was in the 1950s; the 1960s saw the introduction of this important innovation on a major scale; and the 1970s were characterised by its consolidation and adoption as *the* majority process for steelmaking. The history of BOP to the end of the 1960s was described in Meyer and Herregat (*op.cit.*); until then only Japan, among the major steel producing countries, used BOP for three quarters of crude steel production. Apart from pioneering Austria, only the relatively small or new steel industries of the Netherlands and Portugal had comparable diffusion rates.

Table 2.3 shows the shares of the main processes (BOP, electric, open hearth and Thomas) for the years 1969 and 1981 for all European producers and also for the three large non-European steelmaking countries: the United States, Canada and Japan. It also shows crude steel output in this period. For easier demonstration on the same basis, the larger steel producers in the Western world, as well as Austria and Sweden, have been included in chart 2.2, whilst the East European steel producers are shown in chart 2.3.

Because of the complicating effect of electric steel, charts 2.2 and 2.3 approach the spread of BOP by demonstrating the disappearance of the technologies it replaced. The liquidation of the open hearth process had been rapid during the 1970s. By 1981 only small fractions of crude steel were produced in open hearths in Western Europe and presumably this process will disappear entirely within the next two or three years. It may take somewhat longer in North America, where the share of open hearth was still above 10 per cent in 1981. For practical purposes the Thomas process had disappeared by about 1977, except in France where this position was reached by 1981. Electric steelmaking was already important in 1969 (and in many countries much earlier) and it has generally increased its share.

The right-hand sections of charts 2.2 and 2.3 indicate the dissemination of BOP. In the Western countries BOP's advance has been general, with the sole exception of Japan where, in view of electric steel, BOP approached its saturation point as early as the 1960s. Both chart 2.3 and table 2.3 show a different picture for Eastern Europe, however; only there could open hearth production be found in large quantities around 1980. In fact, apart from Bulgaria's relatively new steel industry, BOP accounted for a rather small part of steelmaking, 29 per cent in the USSR, the world's largest producer.

Chart 2.4 shows the differences from country to country even more clearly. Before going into detail, it should be mentioned that, except in the USSR, recession or stagnation characterised the steel industries of the countries included in this chart. In 1981 only in Italy and Austria was steel output comparable to the level reached in 1973 and in the other countries production in 1981 was lower than in 1973. In such circumstances one would expect the older, presumably less efficient, works to be phased out. Continued boom conditions may have prolonged their life by a few years,

Table 2.3. *Crude steel output[a] and steelmaking processes[b]*

	Output		Oxygen		Electric		Open hearth		Thomas[c]
	1969	1981	1969	1981	1969	1981	1969	1981	1969
Major[d] producers, Western Europe									
Belgium	12.8	12.3	45.0	93.7	3.3	6.3	2.2	—	49.5
France	22.5	21.3	22.0	82.5	10.5	17.2	19.8	0.3	47.7
Germany	45.3	43.6	46.0	80.3	9.2	15.8	29.8	3.9	15.0
Italy	16.4	24.8	28.4	48.6	39.9	51.3	31.7	0.1	—
Spain	6.0	12.9	30.1	46.0	36.7	49.3	31.4	4.7	1.8
UK	26.8	15.6	27.6	67.7	18.4	32.3	52.8	—	1.0
Other producers, Western Europe									
Austria	3.9	4.7	69.5	86.5	12.1	10.8	18.4	2.7	—
Denmark	0.5	0.6	—	—	3.9	100.0	96.3	—	—
Finland	1.0	2.4	53.7	88.5	30.1	11.5	16.2	—	—
Luxembourg	5.5	3.8	34.9	100.0	1.8	—	—	—	63.3
Netherlands	4.7	5.5	71.5	94.6	6.9	5.4	21.6	—	—
Norway	0.9	0.8	45.9	51.2	54.1	48.8	—	—	—
Portugal	0.4	0.6	82.2	59.3	17.8	40.7	—	—	—
Sweden	5.3	3.8	32.8	44.6	41.1	52.9	25.4	2.5	0.7
Switzerland	0.5	0.9	—	—	100.0	100.0	—	—	—
Yugoslavia	2.2	4.0	7.7	35.8	19.4	26.4	72.9	37.8	—
Eastern European producers[e]									
Bulgaria	1.5	2.5	52.5	59.2	20.0	25.4	27.5	25.4	—
East Germany[f]	..	7.5	..	10.2	..	28.7	..	60.8	—
Hungary	3.0	3.6	—	14.0	8.4	8.8	91.6	77.3	—
Poland	11.3	15.7	11.4	38.3	7.5	14.0	80.9	47.7	—
Romania	5.5	13.0	18.5	44.5	9.4	19.6	72.2	35.9	—
USSR[f]	110.3	148.5	13.8	29.0[g]	9.0	10.0[g]	75.9	60.4[g]	1.3
Other producers									
Canada	9.4	14.8	1.6	58.6	15.3	27.9	83.1	13.5	—
US	128.0	108.8	42.7	61.1	14.1	27.7	43.2	11.2	—
Japan	82.2	101.7	76.9	75.2	16.7	24.8	6.4	—	—

Source: See chart 2.2.
[a]Million tonnes. [b]Per cent of total crude steel output. [c]Including small quantities of Bessemer in Belgium and France; Bessemer only in Spain, the UK and East Germany. [d]Producing 10 million tonnes or more. [e]Details for Czechoslovakia not available; output in 1981: 15.3 million tonnes. [f]For Thomas, East Germany 1981:0.3, USSR 1979:0.6. [g]1979.

although in view of the marked advantages of BOP that prolongation is unlikely to have been significant.

The management of any innovation is only one problem facing a company and there are many others that must be considered before deciding on such an important investment as the changing of the steelmaking process. It is conceivable that the quota system, as well as local conditions, account for the fact that the older processes were only gradually

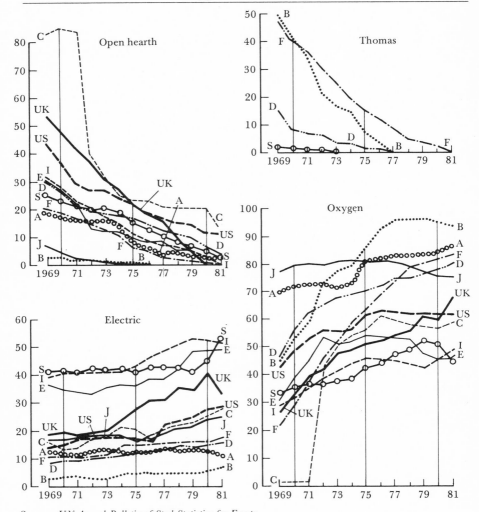

Source: *UN Annual Bulletin of Steel Statistics for Europe*.
Country codes: A – Austria, B – Belgium, C – Canada, D – Germany FR, E – Spain, F – France, I – Italy, J – Japan, S – Sweden, UK – United Kingdom, US – United States.

Chart 2.2 *Steelmaking processes in the main Western producers, 1969–81, percentages in each country's total crude steel production*

dismantled in Germany, surviving as they did for longer there than in some of the other countries, most notably in the United Kingdom. Although starting with a higher share of older technology in 1969 (54 per cent in the United Kingdom as compared with Germany's 45 per cent), open hearth production ended altogether in 1979. Thus, whilst the introduction of BOP

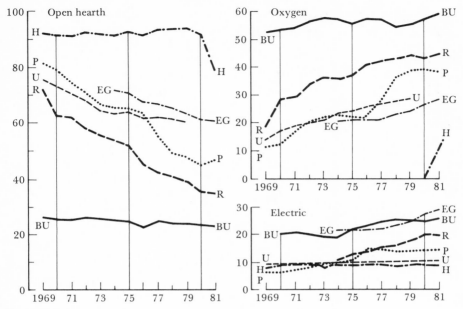

Source: See chart 2.2.

Country codes: BU – Bulgaria; EG – East Germany; H – Hungary; P – Poland; R – Romania; U – USSR.

Chart 2.3 *Steelmaking processes in Eastern Europe, 1969–81, percentages in each country's total crude steel production*
Note changing scales

had not been very speedy in the United Kingdom in the earlier phases, the abandonment of the old technology proceeded with great rapidity in the 1970s. (The British steel industry did have plenty of troubles of other kinds, reflected by the fact that among all the major steelmakers the proportionate fall of steel production from its peak was greatest in the United Kingdom.)

The French industry began with the largest share (68 per cent) of old facilities which were rapidly displaced by BOP during the 1970s. 1980 was the last year of Thomas steel in France, which had accounted for about one half of production in 1969. Had some final users not been over-cautious in their quality considerations before accepting BOP steel, its diffusion might have been more rapid in France. In Belgium the Thomas process was of similar importance and there it was liquidated by 1977, also to be replaced by BOP. Electric steel was already of greater importance in Italy and Sweden at the beginning of our period, partly because of cheap hydro-electricity and partly, in Sweden, because of the high share of special quality steel. In both countries the combination of electric and BOP helped

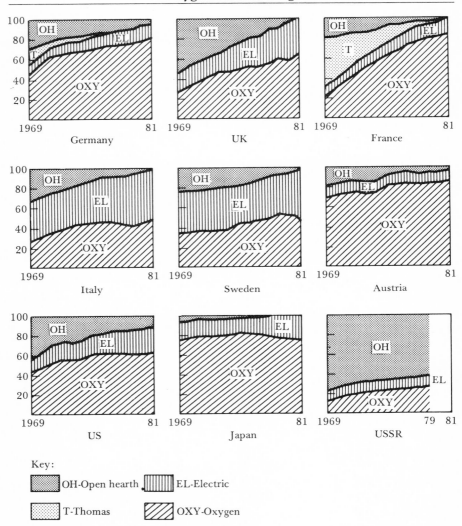

Key:

▨ OH-Open hearth   ▥ EL-Electric

▦ T-Thomas   ▨ OXY-Oxygen

Source: See chart 2.2.
Note: 'OH' also includes small quantities of Bessemer in France, 1969–72; Thomas in Sweden, 1969–72; Bessemer in United Kingdom, 1969–74 and Bessemer in USSR, 1969–79.

Chart 2.4   *Steelmaking processes by country, per cent shares in total crude steel output*

to phase out open hearth. In Austria, where BOP was first introduced, the remaining open hearth production disappeared only slowly but its importance is now only marginal.

In the three giant steelmaking countries developments have been very different. The diffusion of BOP in the United States steel industry has been subject to numerous reports and analyses, some blaming the industry for the relatively slow adoption of the new process, whilst others were more defensive. The fact remains that the share of open hearth was fairly high in 1969 (43 per cent) and, even after gradual reduction, still amounted to 11 per cent in 1981. The thorough study made by Rosegger (*op.cit*) may be referred to for details. It emphasises some of the problems of the United States steel industry and it is probably a fair conclusion to quote his reference to the varying vintages of (and the existence of a number of relatively young) open hearth shops, the techniques developed for improving their performance to fight their suddenly emerging obsolescence, and his finding that 'expectations of cost advantages in the BOP plant *alone* would have constituted a thin reed on which to hang the commitment of a multimillion dollar investment'. He adds that (presumably as from the later 1960s) 'the need for heavy investment in the face of ever tightening environmental control standards may well have hastened the abandonment of older facilities'.

This, incidentally, may be true for other countries as well. In the postwar boom of the 1950s, and even in the 1960s, the capacity of the steel industry in many countries was enlarged and most new integrated works were then built on the open hearth principle; they were still too young to be replaced by BOP soon after the new technique had become ripe for universal application. Moreover, environmental controls, although in many countries less strict than in the United States, might have worked in favour of BOP, acting as a promoting factor to accelerate replacement of the older technologies.

Whilst all this is probably true, the comparison of the United States and Japanese industries nevertheless appears striking. Nowhere was the expansion of the steel industry as rapid as in Japan. The new steelworks boldly adopted the new technology and by 1969 open hearth was almost a matter of the past in Japan and BOP steel accounted for four-fifths of production. It is a point worth pondering to consider to what extent was the higher efficiency of steel production, achieved by the early rapid diffusion of BOP, responsible for the success of the Japanese steel producers, and the more delayed adoption for the relative decline of the United States and West European steel producers.

In the USSR steel has a chapter of its own. Open hearth was, at the end of the 1970s, still the major steelmaking method and it will obviously take a very long time before Soviet steelmakers reach the Western standard, insofar as this particular comparison is concerned.

One additional remark may not be out of place, however. The steel industry has been subjected to exceptional shocks ever since the 1975 recession, to the extent of its becoming a major political issue. Government policies towards maintaining or reducing steel capacities have been different in the various producing countries, even within the European Community. If the policy aimed at capacity reduction, as it did, for example, in the United Kingdom, it obviously contributed to the abandonment of older, less efficient works and thereby to the growth of BOP's importance. Any choice among the possible steelmaking processes (in reality, only between BOP and electric) could be considered, apart from some extraordinary cases, only if sufficient investment capital was available to replace old plant or build new works. Given the unfavourable state of the steel industry, in many countries this depended on state support, usually some form of subsidy from public funds. This competitive subsidisation has become a widespread international feature of the steel industry since the second half of the 1970s, a political rather than an economic factor that, indirectly and to some extent, had an impact on the diffusion indicators of BOP, in whatever way measured, although its quantification is well-nigh impossible.

Another phenomenon was the amalgamation of steelworks, particularly in Germany, with the objective of letting the more progressive companies manage the others; this process presumably resulted in the gradual closure of the less efficient, probably also technologically more backward, plants and might thus have favoured modern production methods. Other protectionist measures, on the other hand, helped the old technology to survive longer than they would otherwise have done in certain areas.

CONCLUSIONS

BOP approached maturity in the 1960s; it has now practically displaced all other methods of integrated steel production in the Western world, except for electric steelmaking. The latter is, however, different in various respects from the BOP-based large works, chiefly in size. These two technologies are likely to remain the methods for producing steel in the foreseeable future.

As a result of technical developments, the range of operation of BOP has been extended to qualities and grades of steel for which it was not applicable some fifteen years ago. In this particular respect BOP has become competitive with electric steel, which was previously the main specialist producer. There is a minimum size for an economic BOP plant which is certainly considerably more than one million and probably around three million tonnes. This leaves room for smaller (mini) plants that operate electric furnaces exclusively and although some of them have more recently been combined with the direct reduction of iron, the mainstay of electric steelmaking remains the scrap. Scrap availability is a basic condition of the economies of electric steel but direct reduction can reduce the need for scrap. Whether in the future we shall see the conventional blast furnace–BOP steelmaking route partly replaced by the

Table 2.4. *Estimated development of steelmaking processes to 2000, percentage of total crude steel production[a]*

	Oxygen	Electric	Open hearth	Thomas and other
European Community				
1967	28	13	34	25
1979/80	72	23	5	—
2000	75	25	—	—
North America				
1967	32	13	55	—
1979/80	61	24	15	—
2000	70	25	5	—
Japan				
1967	67	18	15	—
1979/80	76	24	—	—
2000	80	20	—	—
Soviet Bloc				
1967	9	9	80	2
1979/80	30	12	58	—
2000	53	22	25	—
World[b]				
1967	27	15	51	7
1979/80	52	24	24	—
2000	61	29	10	—

Source: H.M. Aichinger, G.W. Hoffmann and K. Pittel, Die Weltenergiesituation und ihre Auswirkung auf die Eisen– und Stahlindustrie, *Stahl und Eisen*, 101 (1981), p. 191 (955).
[a]Rounded.
[b]Includes producers not shown separately.

newer DRI–electric one will depend, among other things, on the relative costs of coking coal and natural gas and on the success and efficiency of the methods currently being researched for converting low quality coal into an acceptable reducing gas for use in DRI plant. However, this is a complex issue involving many other factors.

Another likely departure in the long term is the continuous manufacture of steel on an automated line in integrated works, following the blast furnace–BOP–continuous casting route. This requires a very high degree of internal control, coordination and organisation. It will mean a continuous flow of material from ore to semi-finished steel, possibly without any major loss of heat underway. Some leading steelmakers have already been experimenting along these lines but many technical problems will have to be solved before the practical application of the idea in large steelworks.

German specialists published a forecast of the development of steelmaking processes in a boldly forward-looking study (see table 2.4). In their view BOP and electric processes will be in exclusive use throughout the world by the year 2000 with the exceptions of the Soviet Bloc and North America. They may be right in the Soviet case but probably not in the American, where the remaining open hearth capacity may be phased out much earlier than 2000, leaving the Soviet Bloc countries alone as operators of the old open hearth technology.

3

CONTINUOUS CASTING OF STEEL

The continuous casting machine replaces three stages of the conventional technology for processing liquid steel into semi-finished products such as slabs, blooms or billets; the casting of ingots, the soaking pit and the blooming mill. Its main advantages lie in increased yield, improved quality, a reduction in floor space, lower investment cost and energy saving. From a rather limited application in the 1950s, continuous casting (CC) was developed and improved gradually during the 1960s but at the end of that decade many technical problems remained to delay its widespread application.[1] Although CC had been mainly applied to special steels, generally in smaller works, around the mid-1960s it was realised that CC machines could be applied on a much larger scale and also for bulk production.

CC, therefore, entered into large-scale integrated steelmaking rather late, much later than had been its adoption in smaller, mostly electric, plants. In the beginning the large plants employed CC mainly for additional capacity and for specific products. Only later were larger CC machines, coupled with BOP converters, employed as central production units. The spread of CC in large works required the introduction of BOP, since the CC machine, to be utilised properly, requires the feeding of liquid metal at regular intervals and this BOP is much better suited to provide than the open hearth or Thomas process. A high degree of coordination between the melting, casting and rolling phases is also needed and this was difficult to achieve in the older works based on other (non-electric) processes without major reorganisation. There were no such difficulties on any major scale in electric plants, indeed, in the more recently built mini-plants CC had already been combined with the furnace in the design phase and the older three-stage system of casting did not even enter into consideration.

Because of its late start, some teething troubles and a number of still unsolved technical problems, the diffusion levels of CC were rather low: in 1970 (see table 3.1) only in Sweden, Japan and Canada was more than 10 per cent of steel continuously cast. This proportion was lower elsewhere, even in the countries that had pioneered the innovation, Germany, Austria and the United Kingdom.

Table 3.1. *Continuous casting of steel, per cent of crude steel output*

	1970	1975	1978	1981		1970	1975	1978	1981
Major producers in Western Europe[a]					*Other producers in Western Europe* (cont)				
Belgium	—	4	21	31	Portugal	..	9	40	38
France	1	13	28	51	Sweden	14	22	29	65
Germany FR	8	24	38	54	Yugoslavia		11	34	43
Italy	4	27	42	51	*East European producers*				
Spain	..	22	29	39	E. Germany	..	8	10	13[b]
UK	2	9	15	32	Hungary	..	21	31	35
Other producers in Western Europe					Poland	..	2	3	4
Austria	8	21	40	62	Romania	..	..	..	21
Denmark	—	13	56	96	USSR	4	7	10	..
Finland	..	76	88	92	*Other producers*				
Luxembourg	—	—	—	7	Canada	11	13	19	32
Netherlands	—	—	—	21	US	4	12	14	21
Norway	..	4	1	—	Japan	11	31	46	71

Source: See Chart 2.2.

[a]Producing 10 million tonnes or more.

[b]1980.

RECENT DEVELOPMENTS IN CC

The original CC machines were vertical and of considerable height (up to 35 metres), which made them difficult to install, especially in existing plants. The first change in the arrangement was made with an arc-type machine in which, after being poured and cooled vertically, the cast strand was bent and then passed through straightening rollers to emerge from the machine horizontally. The further horizontalisation of the CC machine developed naturally, eventually resulting in various almost horizontal arrangements. Apart from consolidating the size of the equipment, the main developments recently have aimed at improving the quality of the steel produced, extending its range and making the CC machine more reliable, as well as raising its productivity. Only some of these developments can be mentioned here.

Electro-magnetic stirring has been introduced to prevent the non-homogeneity that occurs because alloying elements tend to concentrate in the centre of the unevenly solidifying cast steel. As the steel is poured into the mould the problem of re-oxidation emerges. This is now being solved by using a shroud of inert gas (usually argon) around the steel as it is poured, enabling higher grades to be continuously cast, for example, steel for tinplate manufacture. Design developments have solved the problem of steel cracking whilst cooling.

As a consequence of instrumentation better control has been achieved. This is particularly important for CC, which not only requires the regular flow of hot metal but also operates within a narrow temperature range.

All this has made it possible to extend the scope of CC far beyond the limitations still in evidence in the late 1960s: many more types and grades of steel can now be continuously cast but not all of them. There are still grades that cannot be produced by CC, partly because of their shape but mainly because of quality considerations, for example, ball bearing steel and certain qualities of stainless steel.

Although the energy saving advantages of CC, as compared with conventional ingot-casting, are significant (depending on local conditions the saving may be up to three quarters of the energy normally used in this particular phase of steelmaking), our inquiries indicate that even in the recent period of high energy prices these are considered to be of secondary importance, so marked are the cost savings of CC in terms of higher yield and better quality. The productivity of the CC machine depends on the speed of the casting, as well as on the number and size of the strands. Various engineering solutions have raised both, partly by increasing the number of strand outlets attached to the CC machine (though this depends on the semi-product required: up to eight strands for billets but less for others) and partly by applying the CC experience of the non-ferrous metal industries to steel.

Pioneering work on horizontal casting was undertaken at roughly the same time, that is towards the end of the 1960s, by General Motors in the United States and Davy-Ashmore in the United Kingdom, but the search for alternatives to vertical casters also led to the development of other casting processes which offer advantages similar to those attributed to horizontal casters, especially in reduced investment costs. Two such processes have been developed in the United States, CPP, controlled pressure pouring and CRS, controlled rate solidification. These cannot be classified as CC but both permit the direct casting of semi-finished products through the use of pressure pouring into a stationary mould.[2] Although the developers of both processes have attached great hopes to these new methods, dissemination has so far been limited and, insofar as is foreseeable, they are unlikely to have much effect on the further diffusion of CC.

THE DIFFUSION OF CC

Table 3.1 gives the data on the diffusion in most steelmaking countries for some benchmark years and chart 3.1 indicates the annual development since 1975, the starting year for internationally comparable statistics. By 1981 the highest shares (of CC in total crude steel production) were achieved by two smaller producers: Denmark and Finland. Among the larger steelmaking countries Japan takes the lead, just as in the case of BOP, where over 70 per cent of steel went through CC. The over 60 per cent share of Austria and Sweden, two countries where special steels account for a high share of production, may be explained partly by the directions which CC development has taken (first in special steelmaking, then extending into bulk steel and, more recently, in the redevelopment of CC into specialities after having overcome many remaining quality problems). However, this is not the whole explanation, since in Sweden the share of CC for ordinary steel qualities may now, in 1982, be nearly 100 per cent and for specialities 'only' around 70 per cent. The German, French and Italian steel industries are at the same level in CC diffusion. The United Kingdom is much lower in this particular league, in common with other laggards, such as Belgium and the United States.

The bottom section of chart 3.1 shows the same indicator for the USSR and Eastern Europe. As in the case of BOP, these countries (with the apparent exception of Hungary) are far behind the Western level; this is particularly noticeable in the case of the USSR.

The diffusion of CC has definitely been slow. Almost thirty years after the first, admittedly small-scale and primitive, commercial application, its rate was just around 50 per cent for some larger European producers and much lower for other large producing countries (except Japan), although smaller and specialist producers were further ahead. Most experts agree that, apart from financial considerations and the competition amongst major projects for the investment capital available to the steel industry in the post-1973 recessionary period, the main reasons for the delayed spread of this technology lay with quality considerations as well as with the required reorganisation of the internal operations of the steelworks. Recent development has solved most problems that have emerged insofar as quality is concerned. Both internal homogeneity and crack-free surfaces have been achieved, but there are still a few specialities for which CC does not yet seem applicable. There is no doubt, according to the experts, that it is just a question of time before CC becomes universally applicable, perhaps with the exception of niches which will account for a small share of the semi-finished production.

The reorganisation of the internal handling of the metal under processing still remains a problem in many cases, mainly because the existing layout of operations may mean that investment on a significant scale is required. Nevertheless, as CC offers very marked cost savings, it will gradually find its way into a widening section of steel plants.

The spread of BOP and electric steelmaking makes the diffusion of CC easier in two ways. First, new works are likely to have been erected with a CC shop already incorporated and secondly, in existing BOP or electric

Main Western producers

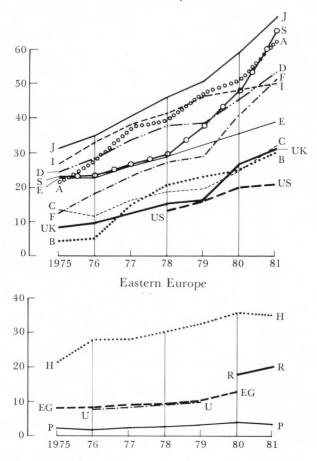

Eastern Europe

Source: See chart 2.2.
Country codes: A – Austria; B – Belgium; C – Canada; D – Germany FR; E – Spain; F – France;
I – Italy; J – Japan; S – Sweden; UK – United Kingdom; US – United States; EG – East Germany;
H – Hungary; P – Poland; R – Romania; U – USSR.

Chart 3.1 *Continuous casting of steel, 1975–81*

plants the reorganisation is relatively much easier than in open hearth
plants, albeit still costly. The installation of CC has occurred parallel with
the expansion of modern steelmaking methods, as indicated by chart 3.2.
Since the latter now account for all steel capacity in many countries and
should gradually approach the same position in others in the coming years,
it is reasonable to assume that the further diffusion of CC will be rapid in
the foreseeable future.

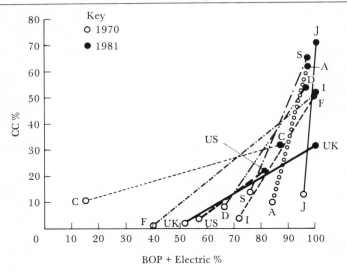

Source: See chart 2.2.
Note: For country codes, see chart 3.1.

Chart 3.2   *The diffusion of modern steelmaking technologies and the spread of
continuous casting, per cent shares in total crude steel production*

The German experience may serve to illustrate that the advantages of
CC are becoming fully utilised. In 1980, a year which saw one of the worst
slumps experienced by the steel industry, the capacity utilisation of CC
machines amounted to 75 per cent, whereas only 65 per cent of crude steel
capacity was utilised.

Further evidence of the superiority of CC is provided by the planned
expansion of this technology. According to the plans of the German steel
industry, CC capacity will reach $38\frac{1}{2}$ million tonnes by 1984, compared
with 27 million tonnes in 1980; this will correspond to 59 per cent of
steelmaking capacity compared with 41 per cent in 1980. In the same year
actual CC production, as distinct from capacity, was 46 per cent of crude
steel output. One study foresees that in ten years time, by the early 1990s,
all but one tenth of German steel will be continuously cast.[3]

In France it is estimated that by the end of this decade CC's share in
crude steel output will reach about 75 per cent. In the United Kingdom
there are active plans to extend CC capacity to 50 per cent of output within
a few years. Finally, according to Swedish steelmakers, it is only a question
of time before CC takes over virtually all steel production and the only
exceptions will be very small quantities of particularly difficult steel
qualitites.

CONCLUSIONS

Various operational problems have caused the diffusion of CC to be relatively slow. By now, however, many, though not all, of them have been successfully overcome and the next few years should see a rapid continued dissemination of this technology. Eventually, apart from some difficult special steel qualities, CC is likely to become an essential part of a modern steel plant, usefully supplementing the up-to-date steelmaking technologies, BOP and the electric furnace, which are much better suited to CC than the earlier open hearth process.

The next development of CC might be the direct casting of steel into the form of plate or sheet. This will further save both energy and capital equipment within the works but is likely to prove technically difficult.

There are two possible technological developments on the horizon that could in due course jeopardise the future of CC, although these are still very much at the research stage: powder technology and rotary continuous casting. The first consists of the creation of a slurry of steel powder which is then rolled into a sheet, sintered and then further rolled into the semi-finished product. If it materialises it will replace casting entirely, whether conventional ingot casting or CC. At present, however, it is only a possible promise for the future. The second retains the basic principle of CC but applies a rotating, wheel-type vessel, already used for the casting of copper and aluminium, to receive the liquid metal, which is then straightened when leaving the rotating wheel. Although its investment costs are much higher than those of conventional CC the high capacity of the rotary system speeds up casting and is said to offer savings in energy and refractory costs. Its future will depend on the outcome of large scale experiments in Germany and Japan.[4]

4

TUNNEL KILNS IN BRICKMAKING

The tunnel kiln is an old invention; the first patent for a kiln of this type was granted in 1840 in Denmark. Its spread in the brick industry is, however, a postwar phenomenon. Until the 1950s the Hoffman type kilns, introduced in the second half of the nineteenth century, dominated the industry. This system consisted of a series of chambers disposed in a circle or in two parallel rows connected by semi-circular or rectangular ends to form a complete circuit. Each chamber had a door to the outside, through which raw dry bricks were introduced and the burnt bricks unloaded. The fire was kindled in one or two chambers and when the bricks there had been burnt, it was moved to an adjacent chamber, continuing along the circuit. Thus, in the Hoffmann kiln, the bricks were stationary and the fire was moving.

In the tunnel kiln the arrangement is just the opposite: the fire is stationary and the bricks move through the firing zone. In this way several significant disadvantages of the Hoffmann kiln (and indeed most other types of kiln) are bypassed. There are three that are most noteworthy. First, working conditions are unpleasant, since in the Hoffmann kiln the operatives have to remove the bricks from chambers which, even after cooling, retain a high temperature. Secondly, the moving fire in the Hoffmann kiln heats and cools the chambers with fluctuations of 1,000–1,100°C in temperature, which wear out the kiln's structure and necessitate frequent and costly maintenance; thirdly, since the huge structure of a Hoffmann kiln is difficult to insulate perfectly, the moving fire may crack the walls and, by drying the floor, cause subsidence in the foundations.

In the case of the tunnel kiln, the loading and unloading of bricks occur outside the kiln in less difficult conditions and the stationary firing zone cuts out much of the damage that a moving fire can cause. The quality of the bricks is better and more uniform and the reject less. However, the tunnel kiln raises other problems. First, capital costs are higher. Secondly, the kiln cars that transport the bricks to and from the firing zone are expensive and require careful maintenance. Thirdly, the burning process has to be much better controlled, usually by instrumentation far more sophisticated than in many of the Hoffmann or other kilns. Finally, the tunnel kiln requires a fuel that is easy to handle and control. The adoption of the tunnel kiln has, therefore, taken place parallel with a general improvement in the degree of mechanisation and automation of the whole productive process (and not just the burning phase).

Two important factors hindered the rapid diffusion of the tunnel kiln. First, the lifetime of a kiln is long; Hoffmann kilns can be used for fifty, or even more, years if properly maintained; they are written off considerably faster and once their depreciation costs are no longer charged to current output they produce bricks cheaply. Secondly, the tunnel kiln is not used for burning bricks made of clay with a high carbon content since the latter makes fire control difficult, vastly reduces the savings in energy costs that the tunnel kiln offers and makes the higher investment cost of the tunnel kiln unjustifiable.

The role of the fuel supply is ambiguous. Solid fuels are less suitable in a tunnel kiln than in other kilns and older works used to coal, especially those in locations favourable to its transportation, might have retained their kilns in preference to a tunnel kiln in view of the disadvantages of coal in the latter. On the other hand, the generally easy availability of cheap oil and gas elsewhere in the postwar period has indirectly favoured the dissemination of the tunnel kiln.

At the end of the 1960s, the tunnel kiln was not yet the dominant feature of many countries' brick industry which it is today. In the earlier study[1] there were two estimates of its diffusion, both based on samples, indicating very large variations among countries. The first estimate measured the share of bricks made in tunnel kilns in total brick output and in Europe varied between 9 per cent in the United Kingdom and 78 per cent in Germany and Sweden. The second estimate introduced the concept of a technological ceiling, which excluded two types of brick production from total brick output: first, bricks made of clay with a high carbon content (such as the fletton bricks in Britain) and secondly, all bricks produced in smaller works. Smaller works were those producing not more than ten and fifteen million bricks a year, depending on the conditions in the particular country, on the grounds that even one tunnel kiln produced larger quantities in normal operations. (It is, of course, debatable whether this second restriction is a technological or an economic one.) The diffusion estimates, with respect to the technological ceilings thus defined, naturally showed higher values, ranging from 33 per cent in the United Kingdom to over 80 per cent in Germany, Sweden and Austria.

The outstanding feature of the original inquiry was the relatively very low diffusion of the tunnel kiln in the United Kingdom. The diffusion pattern in the countries covered was submitted to various tests based on theoretical considerations in an attempt to explain the differences. These included the concentration of production (that is, the presence of small and medium-sized firms), the rate of return, the uncertainty of demand, the outlook for the need for new capacity, the fuel situation, the age of existing kilns, the fluctuation in demand for bricks, the quality requirements and so on. Britain's low rate of diffusion appeared to be the result of a number of factors, such as the low concentration of non-fletton production, the varied quality of bricks required (in view of the more widespread use of bricks and the fact that the tunnel kiln is less flexible in re-setting to another variety than other kilns), the preponderance of coal (an argument weakened by the comparison with Germany, equally well endowed with coal), and the competition from cheap fletton bricks which are distributed nationwide. The latter might have been one of the decisive factors; another was the fact that in the mid-1950s the average age of kilns in the British sample was less than half of that in any of the other countries. Moreover, there was no need to add to national capacity, partly because of the existing production potential and partly because prospects for new building were much less favourable in Britain than on the Continent.

RECENT DEVELOPMENT OF THE TECHNOLOGY

While both the principle and the practice of operating the tunnel kiln have remained unchanged during the 1970s, there have been a number of developments, among which three are worth mentioning. First, there has been a general trend towards further instrumentation of the burning process and of the whole operation of the kiln. Secondly, the mechanical loading of raw bricks onto the kiln cars transporting them to the firing zone has been perfected; the same can be said of the unloading of the burned bricks at the far end of the kiln, although this operation might not yet have reached the same stage as the mechanisation of loading.

Thirdly, various steps have been made to improve the energy economy of the tunnel kiln, particularly stimulated by the steep increase in energy prices after 1973, such as better insulation and more frequent auditing of energy use aimed at discovering leaks and reducing heat losses by various methods of heat recycling. Rising energy prices encouraged more powerful additional measures, such as the injection of oxygen to speed up the burning process and the switch to fuels that are easiest to handle and control, mainly gas.

In the original report it was stated: 'In 1955, oil and gas were already being used very widely in the Swedish, American and Italian brick industries, as opposed to those in Germany, the United Kingdom and, to a lesser extent, Austria, which were still based on coal . . . By the mid-1960s, however, while all six [countries] were using relatively more liquid fuels than previously, Germany, and particularly the United Kingdom, were still very dependent on solid fuels'. This situation has changed radically during the 1970s. As chart 4.1 indicates, by 1974 89 per cent of the tunnel

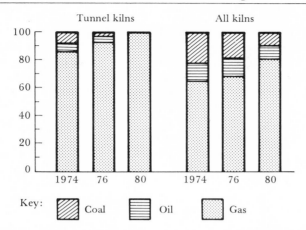

Source: H.W.H. West and C.N. Walley, 'Fuel usage in the manufacture of building bricks', three reports with the same title in *Technical Notes 261* (1976), *279* (1978) and *337* (1982), British Ceramic Research Association, Stoke-on-Trent.
[a]By number of continuous and intermittent kilns.

Chart 4.1   *Fuel usage in the United Kingdom non-fletton brick industry, per cent distribution*[a]

kilns in the British brick industry used gas; by 1980 this had become the exclusive fuel used in these kilns. A similar tendency characterises the whole non-fletton industry where by 1980 only one tenth of all kilns used coal, and a similar proportion used oil. (These were, of course, non-tunnel kilns.)

In the British case the spread of gas was related to the general increase in gas usage, mainly owing to the availability of North Sea gas, the coming on stream of the nationwide gas pipeline network, and the relatively low price of natural gas. However, the trend was similar in Germany too, the only difference being that because gas there was less abundantly available and perhaps less favourably priced, the switch from coal was in the direction partly of gas and partly of fuel oil, which was almost as easy to control as gas and much more convenient to handle than coal. According to German estimates, the energy use of the brick industry in that country consists of 40–60 per cent oil (about two-thirds heavy and one-third light fuel oil), 30–50 per cent gas and only about 10 per cent coal. The trends which have been observed are a decreasing share of oil, the rising importance of gas, especially of liquid gases and probably also the growing use of coal pulverised into fine coal powder. Nevertheless, even in this modified form coal firing presents the old problems: the ash influences brick quality and the environmental pollution of coal is significantly worse than that of gas or even oil firing.

In France too gas made headway, mainly at the expense of fuel oil. In 1980, 55 per cent of the industry's energy consumption was in gas, compared with about one third in the early 1970s.

Another effect of the changing energy situation has been the increased mixing with the clay of materials that act as fuel, such as sawdust, expanded polystyrene, and so on. These not only reduce the quantity of energy required in the kiln but also increase the porosity of the product and thereby its insulating capacity.

There have been developments in the Hoffmann-type kilns also. In the traditional Hoffmann transverse arch kilns the application of insulated steel doors and other minor improvements have raised thermal efficiency. Although very few new kilns have been built on the Hoffmann principle, one development (in Britain) resulted in the flat-arched (also called suspended roof) continuous kiln. This is highly insulated and, with built-in heat recovery, its energy efficiency is markedly higher than that of the earlier Hoffmann kilns (and even of some tunnel kilns).[2]

Energy has always been a very important element in the costs of brick production and its input, especially in the larger and more advanced works, has always been subject to continuous monitoring. This is especially true of tunnel kilns. It was therefore unlikely that the specific energy use could fall suddenly and drastically. Nevertheless, there has been a marked reduction in energy use, as table 4.1 demonstrates from the example of the British experience (which can be taken as a guide to the minimum of changes in the brick industries of other countries too). The figures also indicate the advantage, from the point of view of energy use, of the tunnel kiln.

Further improvement in the energy efficiency of kilns, especially the tunnel kiln, continues to be a main objective of research and development. Evidence of this may be seen in the large number of academic and other articles published in the trade journals.[3]

Table 4.1. *Gross energy requirements for facing and engineering bricks in the United Kingdom, index numbers of therms per tonne*

Tunnel kiln = 100	1974	1976	1980	*1974 = 100*	1974	1976	1980
Tunnel kilns	100	100	100	Tunnel kilns	100	99	93
Chamber kilns	134	135	133	All kilns	100	100	91
Hoffmann kilns	117	113	123				

Source: See chart 4.1.

THE DIFFUSION OF THE TUNNEL KILN

The information collected in the course of this inquiry relates to the whole of the brick industries of Germany, France, Italy and Sweden. For the United Kingdom the survey reports of the British Ceramic Research Association (*op.cit.*) have been used which in the three years they were conducted (1974, 1978 and 1980) covered 80, 81 and 90 per cent, respectively, of national output. The results are shown in table 4.2.

Another way of measuring diffusion is to illustrate changes in the numbers of tunnel kilns and table 4.3 shows these changes for France and Italy. In Germany in 1982 there were about 400 tunnel kilns and some 20 Hoffmann kilns; since 1970 all new kilns have been tunnels. In Sweden,

Table 4.2 *The share of tunnel kilns in brick production, percentages*

	1970	1975	1980
France	60	80	90
Germany	50	60	90[a]
Italy	45–50[b]	70	90
Sweden	. .	. .	95[c]
UK[d]	42	57	72

Source: NIESR Inquiry.
[a] 'At least 95 per cent by 1982'.
[b] TK was not yet considered applicable to certain types of bricks in 1970; the diffusion rate was 45 per cent related to the whole production and 50 per cent if the 'not applicable' quantity is excluded.
[c] 'Virtually the whole production'.
[d] 1970 is estimated on the basis of the original report, 1975 and 1980 from BCRA reports. The data relate to facing and engineering bricks, that is, excluding flettons and non-fletton common bricks since some three quarters of the latter, chiefly in Scotland, also consist of high-carbon clay.

Table 4.3. *Number of tunnel kilns*

	1970	1975	1982
France	100	160	170
Italy	150	200	240[a]

Source: Inquiry.
[a] 1981.

where the brick industry has shrunk considerably in the 1970s, at the time of the original study at the end of the 1960s 22 out of a total of 35 kilns were tunnel kilns; in 1982 there were 14 kilns in operation and all except one (a Hoffmann) are tunnels.

In the United Kingdom the situation is different. The 1980 BCRA survey counted 164 kilns for non-fletton building bricks of which only 51 were tunnel kilns; the others were: 15 Hoffmann, 24 chamber, 39 intermittent down-draught, 16 shuttle kilns and 19 clamps. The capacity of many of these kilns is, of course, much smaller than and often only a fraction of that of tunnel kilns. The number of operational non-tunnel kilns is reflected in the diffusion rate of the United Kingdom, which is considerably lower than that in the other countries.

These diffusion figures should be viewed against the background of the strong and long recession in the building and construction trades in practically all countries. The wider application of concrete instead of bricks has further depressed demand for bricks in some countries (for example, Germany). In the United Kingdom the recession was perhaps more marked than elsewhere. Brick production in 1981 was not much more than half that in 1972–3 (see chart 4.2) but the recession was not confined to Britain; in France brick output in 1980 was 21 per cent below that in 1970 and in Germany it fell 25 per cent by 1981 from its previous peak in 1972.

There may be at least two reasons why the role of tunnel kilns grows in importance in recessionary periods. First, they are more efficient and it is reasonable to assume that the least efficient kilns will be the first to be taken out of production when times are difficult (unless they are totally written off and can therefore compete for a while, despite being obsolete). Secondly, firms with better financial backing and/or management are more likely to survive the slump than others; most probably, these firms already operate tunnel kilns. Moreover, these successful firms often take over other, usually smaller, brickmakers if they get into trouble and may close down, temporarily at least, their (usually non-tunnel kiln) plants. Thus, the upsurge in the share of tunnel kilns in production may be only partly the outcome of a deliberate action of operating them in preference to other kilns, or replacing other older kilns by tunnel kilns and partly the result of ownership and operating practices.

This process of concentration is not new. In Britain, the number of brick plants fell from 1,150 in 1938 to 780 in 1951, operated by 600 firms; by 1976 the number of plants was only 248, controlled by 128 companies[4] and a more recent survey puts the number of independent companies in 1979 as low as 60.[5] The fletton industry is totally concentrated in the hands of the London Brick Company, whilst the non-fletton industry is basically one of mainly medium-sized producers where the top twelve firms account for only 40 per cent of production.

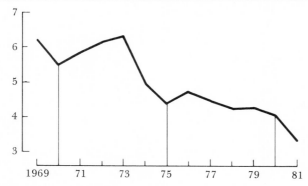

Source: Department of the Environment.

Chart 4.2 *Clay bricks production in the United Kingdom, thousand millions*

Elsewhere the concentration process was also noticeable. In France, for example, the number of establishments in this industry fell from 404 in 1970 to 260 in 1980, when one quarter of them accounted for 80 per cent of sales. The number of German brickworks also declined from 506 in 1970 to 284 in 1981 when 5 per cent of the enterprises produced 35 per cent of the industry's output.

Concentration favours the adoption of tunnel kilns since the tunnel kiln sets minimum limits on production that may be higher than the output of some small firms. Furthermore, the larger companies have easier access to investment capital, which is higher for tunnel kilns than for other kilns.

The recession has also affected the product mix of output, in view of the different requirements of new building and maintenance and repair. In France, for example, 82 per cent of production consisted of bricks (the rest roofing tiles) in 1970 but only 73 per cent in 1980. In the British sample, on the other hand, non-fletton facing and engineering bricks, for which diffusion has been calculated, accounted for 36 per cent of production in 1970 and 46 per cent in 1980. The change in the product mix varied from country to country but it is unlikely to have affected the diffusion of the tunnel kiln or the validity of its international comparison.

One factor that has to be borne in mind is the supply of labour. The handling of bricks in Hoffmann and other types of kilns was originally manual. Methods for mechanical loading, at least for the Hoffmann kiln, have been available for some time but were not yet generally applied when the tunnel kiln became more popular during the two decades following the war. The heavy physical work and high temperatures made the manual operations in a brick kiln one of the most burdensome of factory-type manual labour. One of the important advantages of the tunnel kiln was that it could ease this burden. In fact, in Sweden according to our Inquiry, 'it became impossible to get workers for the old type of heavy work' and the tunnel kiln offered the way out of this impasse. It is not possible to provide much evidence about the supply of labour in Britain. However, the pressure for change seems to have been less marked. The tunnel kiln requires less manual labour and the wish to retain jobs may have been stronger than the wish for easier working conditions. Probably the average age of workers is higher in Britain and those workers were used to the heavy work and did not feel the need for change. Moreover, throughout the 1970s it was easier for the British industry to attract the labour it needed than it was in Germany and France (in spite of the presence of Gastarbeiter in Germany and immigrants in France) so that there was less need for British employers to offer better working conditions.

The Italian, Swedish and German view is that any type or quality of bricks can be produced in tunnel kilns. The French attitude is more complicated. There are still some 50 Hoffmann kilns, mainly in small plants in the North of France, making solid common bricks but these are out-of-date plants producing small quantities and sooner or later will either modernise or disappear. However, French employers admit the justification of a few 'intermittent' kilns, operated largely by craftsmen, for making tiles for flooring and decorative purposes as well as ornamental ware. No such need seems to arise in Germany: practically all ornamental clayware is imported.

The attitude of the British industry is rather different. Apart from the carbon content of the clay which makes the tunnel kiln unsuitable for fletton bricks, the difference may stem from building practices in Britain, where, in contrast to most continental countries, there is a preference for a generous application of bricks in residential and other buildings and their use for ornament and decoration. It is argued that certain ranges of bricks, such as stocks and blue bricks, cannot be made in tunnel kilns, for a variety of reasons. But since these special bricks are not made in large quantities they cannot account for the apparent backwardness of the British industry in introducing the tunnel kiln, compared with other countries. The labour situation, briefly mentioned above, may explain a small part of the difference. The following are the most likely additional reasons. First, some old kilns are totally written off, so that production, with no capital cost, is cheap and competitive. Secondly, some producers enjoy a quasi-monopolistic position in a narrow local area, strengthened by the increased transportation costs for bricks, which are in any case high. Thirdly, some producers, especially the small firms, have no money to build a tunnel kiln, especially not in a time of recession and with poor prospects for a building boom.

CONCLUSIONS

The tunnel kiln has become dominant during the 1970s and in many countries its application has reached or is approaching saturation. Among the countries covered the only exception is the United Kingdom, where, for various reasons, older types of kilns are still operating in large numbers. Apart from small niches, special products or particular conditions, that will account for only a small fraction of production, it is just a question of time before practically all non-fletton bricks will be fired in tunnel kilns. Any new brick kiln will probably be a tunnel kiln, wherever possible gas-fired. Only in Britain have experiments been carried out on a serious competitor, the suspended roof (flat arched) continuous kiln, developed from the Hoffmann kiln. Despite its success it has, however, remained an isolated case so far.

The technology of the tunnel kiln is fully mature; it is nevertheless likely to be further developed. The most likely target for development is to be found in the further improvement of the kiln's energy efficiency by better control of the burning method, oxygen dosage, and so on. Another departure, further in the future, may be in the direction of more lightweight construction that will permit closing down the kiln for a shorter working week. A closer combination of the brick shaping–drying–burning process, going beyond the present arrangement in the form of some kind of continuous line, is also being discussed in the trade journals but at present is still a promise for the future.

5

SHUTTLELESS LOOMS

By the end of the 1960s shuttleless looms had passed the take off phase but had not moved far along the upward slope of the diffusion curve which any successful innovation has to climb before reaching wider dissemination.[1] Its advantages were already clear, although certain disadvantages still could not be denied. It was obvious that the shuttleless loom (SL) was a labour-saving piece of equipment of considerable importance, that it produced fabrics of high and uniform quality and that it was a significant bonus to the labour force in that it reduced noise, that troublesome environmental nuisance of the shuttle looms.

There were also disadvantages found at the time by the international survey of textile manufacturers. Firms had both general and specific reasons why they did not install them. Financial problems, low profits and the uncertainty of the textile market were all factors hindering the speedy adoption of this innovation in general. More specific reasons were also given, however, such as the limited flexibility of SLs, the rather primitive selvedge of the fabrics woven on them, their unsuitable technical nature for certain types of fabrics and non-standardised products, and the high capital cost of the new machines that made investing in them questionable when the then present looms were adequate, even if they were not yet entirely written off. There were also limitations to the number of colours that could be woven and, on certain types of SLs, to the width of the fabric. Finally, SLs required a higher quality, stronger, yarn than was generally available at competitive prices in the years prior to the late 1960s.

At that time the projectile system (and within it the Sulzer loom) was probably the most technically mature among the four main categories of SLs. The rapier loom, although already developed technically, only began to achieve limited acceptance whilst the air and water jet looms were some way behind in their development and undergoing teething troubles.

By the 1950s and 1960s, the textile manufacturers in the advanced countries were facing gradually strengthening competition from the young textile industries that had sprung up after the war in the developing areas of the world as well as from some other countries which already had fairly large textile sectors before the war which were exporting on an increasing scale. It was an open secret that cheap labour was the key to the latters' success and the more enlightened companies in the established textile industries of the industrial countries looked at SLs as a means of withstanding the keen competition, in view of their greatly reduced labour requirements.

In terms of labour, SLs continued the trend to a reduction of working hours per unit of output, a trend going back to the middle of the 18th century (see chart 5.1) when some 300–400 hours were needed to weave 100 metres of cloth. The various innovations, gradually reducing this to about one hour on an automatic shuttle loom, went hand in hand with innovations of similar importance in spinning. A technical jump in one of the two main sectors of the textile industry often encouraged inventors in the other sector, indeed almost necessitated further advance there. SLs further reduced the working hours required to weave the same quantity to well under one hour.

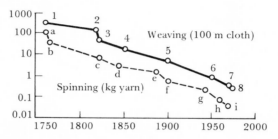

Source: H.W. Krause, Zukunftsperspektiven textiler Fertigung, *Textil-Praxis*, 1970, Heft 4, pp. 195–200; Sulzer AG, Winterthur.

Key: *Weaving* 1 hand loom; 2 flying shuttle; 3 mechanical loom; 4 multiloom weaving; 5 Northrop pirn changer; 6 automatic loom; 7 jet; 8 projectile.

Spinning a spinning wheel; b Hargreaves; c spinning jenny; d mule; e self-actor; f el. ring frame; g ring frame; h automatic ring frame; i rotorspinning.

Chart 5.1 *Human labour requirements in weaving and spinning, 1750–1980, working hours, semilog scale*

The automatic shuttle loom, with up-to-date equipment but without electronic shuttle flight control, left much to be desired. As one major company, approached in the course of this inquiry, summed it up: 'it has too many setting points and is the least reliable weaving machine'. SLs have many fewer setting points, are very reliable and need a fraction of the attention paid to shuttle looms, with the result that one weaver can be put in charge of a large group of SLs (sometimes more than forty).

This is very different from the earlier situation where one weaver could not handle more than a very small number of machines because of the frequent yarn breakages. With its much higher speed and larger width the SL's productivity was vastly superior to that of the shuttle loom. In addition, the improved quality, the reduced cost of weft preparation and the low maintenance costs, promised the swift spread of the new equipment throughout the whole textile industry.

As will be discussed below, this has indeed been the case. While our study covers the cotton-type weaving section of the industry only, the diffusion in other sectors, for example wool, has also been rapid. In one sense only were SLs a disappointment. They did not save the textile industries in the advanced countries which, on the whole, continued to decline, at least relatively. One reason for this was that quite a few of the textile producers in the developing areas of the world had also discovered the superiority of SLs and invested, some of them heavily, in the new equipment.

RECENT DEVELOPMENTS

The basic principles did not change much during the 1970s; nevertheless, all categories of SLs had developed significantly from the end of the 1960s, mainly in the direction of higher speed, improved performance, better servicing and further noise reduction.

Views expressed by German firms show clearly the changes that increased the speed of SLs. In the 1960s the typical speed of weft insertion in all categories was 400–600 metres a minute, with the air jet machines standing out at about 700 metres a minute. These speeds would be unacceptable today. Maximum performances (although the averages are lower) are now 1,400–1,500 metres a minute for the jets and 1,100 metres a minute for the projectile and rapier types. In addition, at least for some of the main types such as projectile looms, the manufacturers expect a lifetime that is unusually long in mechanical engineering. This is an advantage from the point of view of maintenance and durability, though it will make it more difficult to replace these looms by even newer, more advanced models.

Technical development has probably been most rapid in the case of air jet looms. A second generation air jet loom was introduced by a Czech company at the very beginning of the 1970s, its principal structural change being that the air jet was led in channels that helped to increase the speed and also the width of the machine that was now extended to 2.30 metres. About the middle of the 1970s further progress was made with the application of relays along the width of the cloth; this meant that the width of the machines could be enlarged to 3.30 metres without reducing the speed. These changes have made the air jet loom applicable for the production of wide staple goods (an area where the projectile looms, for example the Sulzer, had great advantages before these air jet developments) although the colour limitations of the air jet have not been materially eased. Much research has been undertaken to further reduce the noise level of SLs. This same objective had been followed by makers of shuttle looms, although at a much higher noise level.

Technical improvements have also raised the speed of water jets but these remain handicapped by the need for either hydrophobic (water-repellent) yarn, or the subsequent drying of the woven cloth. Despite the need for additional equipment for cleaning the highly polluted water before recycling, many consider the water jet currently superior for the weaving of pure nylon or polyester yarn in simple construction, but further development work now in progress on the air jet suggests that within the next few years the positions might be reversed.

Fabrics having mixed wefts to pattern, or those with structural effects or many colours are, and probably will continue to be, woven on the usually narrower rapier looms. Some of these can handle fourteen colours, whereas projectile looms, which provide the closest alternative for these types of weaving, can only handle up to eight colours. The projectile looms, such as the Sulzer, reached maturity earlier than the jets; their main development has been to almost treble their speed in the past fifteen years. Some evidence for the growing popularity of air jet looms lies in the fact that over the last five years or so virtually all important producers of looms have begun to manufacture two types, one of which is an air jet loom.

The range of products that SLs can cover has also been significantly extended. Nowadays the types of textile fabrics for which SLs are unsuitable are limited to technical and speciality fabrics, such as industrial textiles, heavy belting, felt, or too narrow/too wide fabrics; but efforts are now being made to enable such fabrics to be woven in one of the various types of SLs. It should be noted, however, that whilst there is at least one SL type suitable for most fabrics, any one type would not necessarily serve all possible requirements. Well informed spokesmen take the view that if conventional shuttle looms can handle 100 per cent of production rapier and projectile looms can manage 92–95 per cent, airjets about 50 per cent (but this share is on the increase), and waterjets about 10 per cent. They add that instead of saying 'can' one could actually say that they 'do'.

The number of SL producers has grown appreciably in the past ten to fifteen years. At the time of our original report at the end of the 1960s, only a handful of textile manufacturers offered SLs; at present the investor faces a large variety, some of them from developing countries. Six different companies offer SLs from Japan, three each from Italy, Switzerland and Taiwan, at least two each from France and Germany and one each from Belgium, Brazil, Czechoslovakia, Spain and the United Kingdom. The number in the United States, the USSR and China, is not known. Although there are differences in the quality and performance of these machines, all are certainly shuttleless. It has been reported, for example, that the Chinese make relatively simple SLs and have delivered many of them to developing countries in Africa. It is also known that some factories update their shuttle looms by using kits that change weft insertion, converting them into simple SLs, and this is becoming increasingly important.

In this context, the decline of the British textile machinery industry deserves a mention. In the mid-1950s Britain's share in world exports of textile machinery was over 30 per cent (earlier it had been even higher); by 1975 it was no more than about 10 per cent. Between 1963 and 1975, the United Kingdom share fell from 17 to 10 per cent, the German share rose to 35 per cent by 1972 and, after a decline, remained unchanged at 30 per cent until 1975, but the Swiss share rose to 16 per cent, the Japanese increased and matched the United Kingdom share at about 10 per cent, and the French and Italian shares also rose during the period, although at a somewhat lower level. According to Rothwell,[2] the decline of British textile machinery was probably not due in the main to price differences but rather to technological factors. Although SLs account for only a part of textile machinery, the reasons why United Kingdom textile companies purchased foreign-built machinery in the 1970–6 period convey an important message. Altogether 95 textile companies, including the major ones, bought foreign-built machinery during that period and no more than 4 per cent of them mentioned that the foreign machinery was cheaper. The other reasons that were given were that the machinery in question was not available from United Kingdom companies (27 per cent), that it was not matched by a suitable British made alternative (11 per cent), that the foreign machine was superior in overall performance, design and efficiency (32 per cent), that it was technically more advanced in design (13 per cent), was backed by better after-sales service ($5\frac{1}{2}$ per cent) and that it was better in regard to specific user requirements ($3\frac{1}{2}$ per cent).

These were all non-price factors and amply justify Rothwell's closing remark that 'technical innovation has been, and is, an extremely important determinant in the export competitiveness of textile machinery'. He went on to say that outside certain 'new' machinery areas (such as texturising, carpet tufting and so on), the British industry has generally been less innovative than its main European rivals.

The shift of the textile industries from the advanced countries to the developing areas has continued at a steady pace. Between 1973 and 1980 the share of European consumption taken by non-Community imports rose from 21 per cent to 44 per cent.[3] Some of the textile consumption takes the form of ready-made clothing; the EC's external trade balance for clothing alone has been in deficit since the 1960s and for the whole (textiles–clothing) sector became negative in 1975 'and the deficit is growing year by year'.

THE DIFFUSION OF SHUTTLELESS LOOMS

Because of this geographical shift in the industry, particular attention has also been paid to the diffusion of SLs outside the advanced countries. Table 5.1 contains the information that we were able to collect on this and shows, for the continents, for all OECD countries and a large number of other countries, the following indicators: the share of SLs in a) 1981 textile machinery shipments to the countries shown; b) the cumulative shipments for the years 1974–81; c) total automatic looms installed at the beginning of 1981; and d) the number of all looms (including non-automatic looms) at the beginning of 1980 and the share in this total of shuttleless and non-automatic looms.

No great importance should be attached to the situation in any one year but the 1981 shipments statistics are nevertheless of some interest. The new looms delivered to North American and European (including East European) countries consisted almost wholly of SLs; the share of shuttle looms was 10 per cent or less. About two thirds of the new looms in South America and one third of those in Africa were SLs and the share in Asia, where one half of the world's looms are concentrated, was also one third. Altogether, 61 per cent of all new looms in the world were SLs.

In most industrial countries the share of SLs was over 90 per cent and in many of them very nearly 100 per cent, with three notable exceptions, Japan, Switzerland and the United Kingdom. Japan is a special case in view of the great importance of silk weaving which, in these statistics, is treated together with cotton type weaving. The parallel between Switzerland and the United Kingdom reminds one of the time when 'cotton was king' and the keenest competitor of the then ruling British cotton manufacturers was the Swiss cotton trade, mainly with finer and specialised products. This product mix might explain the Swiss case, since otherwise the Swiss textile machinery manufacturers are among the world leaders, and to an extent also that of the United Kingdom, although conservatism might have played a greater part in the latter.

In many of the East European countries (including the USSR) the newly installed looms also consisted entirely of SLs; the Czechoslovak case is very similar to that of Switzerland, another country with a highly developed textile machinery industry producing sophisticated fabrics. Among the developing countries the advance of SLs is similarly obvious, although many still installed new shuttle looms.

More meaningful than just one year's data are the figures that indicate the cumulative installations in the eight years ending in 1981. The relative picture (in the second column of table 5.1) is similar to that for 1981 alone in many respects, but different in others. Noteworthy is the very high percentage of SLs in Eastern Europe (99–100 per cent in the USSR, East Germany and Bulgaria). The position of the United Kingdom, with 60 per cent of the cumulative shipments in SLs, is nearer to the majority of the industrial countries, but the lagging is still apparent behind most other OECD countries with a share of well over 70 per cent, or behind Germany

Table 5.1. *Shuttleless looms:[a] selected indicators*

| | Per cent share of SL in | | | All looms installed at 1 January '80[c] | | |
| | | | | 000s | Per cent share[d] | |
	1981 ship-ments	1974–81 cumulative shipments	Total automatic[b] looms installed at 1 January '81		Shuttle-less	Non-automatic
Germany	99	74	16	38	9	1
UK	66	60	29	35	22	22
France	96	77	23	37	16	8
Italy	91	81	16	47	12	3
Sweden	100	76	64	1	35	45
US	99	73	18	224	16	—
Japan	58	26	12	306	4	61
Africa	32	18	6	114	4	15
N and C America	94	68	18	304	13	3
S America	61	43	6	226	3	37
Asia and Oceania	34	17	4	1414	2	43
Western Europe	91	75	18	328	11	13
Eastern Europe	90	80	23	470	18	27
World	61	44	12	2855	7	31
Countries with over 100,000 looms at 1 January '80						
Brazil	35	22	2	150	1	51
China	100	16	1–	490	1–	41
India	3	4	1	207	1–	78
USSR	100	100	30	322	23	23
Countries with 20,000 to 100,000 looms						
Egypt	24	8	1	40	1	20
Mexico	85	69	21	52	7	16
Argentina	100	74	15	25	13	12
Hong Kong	100	66	1	30	3	—
Indonesia	40	11	3	68	2	38
Iran	22	12	6	23	5	15
South Korea	1	9	2	75	2	—
Pakistan	—	14	2	33	1	18
Philippines	—	14	4	21	3	n.a.
Taiwan	34	22	18	57	11	8
Thailand	73	2	1–	58	1–	10
Czechoslovakia	51	71	4	32	3	21
East Germany	100	99	8	38	4	48
Poland	100	90	35	33	9	39
Portugal	76	57	10	35	4	43
Spain	97	58	12	28	14	14
Turkey	75	38	4	40	2	18
Yugoslavia	100	88	9	21	8	12
Other OECD countries with 10,000 to 20,000 looms						
Canada	100	78	9	12	9	—
Belgium	99	80	8	18	7	8
Australia	96	73	16	4	14	13
Austria	93	82	19	5	15	1
Denmark	—	90	22	1	19	17

Table 5.1 *(cont.)*

	Per cent share of SL in			All looms installed at 1 January '80[c]	Per cent share[d]	
	1981 ship-ments	1974–81 cumulative shipments	Total automatic[b] looms installed at 1 January '81	000s	Shuttle-less	Non-automatic
Finland	96	86	16	2	13	6
Greece	86	65	21	9	17	17
Netherlands	100	82	39	5	29	3
Switzerland	77	79	13	7	11	—

Source: International Textile Manufacturers Federation, Zurich. Partly estimated. In the various size-categories the countries are listed in alphabetical order by continent.
[a]In cotton-type weaving.
[b]Automatic looms at least 75 cm wide; excludes non-automatic looms.
[c]Including non-automatic (hand) looms.
[d]The remainder consists of automatic shuttle looms.

(74 per cent) and France (77 per cent) or Italy (81 per cent). Yet the United Kingdom share of SLs in the total number of *automatic* looms installed at the beginning of 1981 was higher than in any of the latter three countries at 29 per cent. Only in some East European countries and in a few of the smaller European countries was the share of SLs in all automatic looms higher than in the United Kingdom.

For the United Kingdom, the three large European countries and the United States these different measures of diffusion are shown in chart 5.2.

The above assessment of the share of SLs in the total stock was based on automatic looms alone. However, there are still a very large number of non-automatic (including hand-) looms in operation in various parts of the world, altogether almost one third of the total loom stock. Information on the latter is shown in the last three columns of table 5.1. Most of the non-automatic looms are in Asia, South America and Eastern Europe.[4] Among the advanced countries the percentage of non-automatic looms is very high in the United Kingdom. Apart from the special case of Japan, because of silk, there are only two OECD countries where this share is higher than Britain's 22 per cent, in Portugal and in the very small Swedish industry. In Germany it is 1 per cent, in France 8 per cent, in Italy 3 per cent, in Switzerland and the United States zero (see chart 5.3). The question is therefore: why are so many non-automatic, and therefore presumably obsolete, looms still installed, although not necessarily operating, in the United Kingdom?

A comparison of the national statistics of France and the United Kingdom (see chart 5.4) does not indicate any great difference in the share

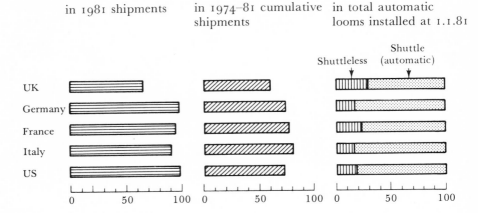

in 1981 shipments   in 1974–81 cumulative   in total automatic
                           shipments   looms installed at 1.1.81

Source: *International Cotton Industry Statistics*, ITMF, Zurich.
[a]75cm and wider automatic looms only, in the cotton system.

Chart 5.2 The share of shuttleless looms in all automatic looms[a]

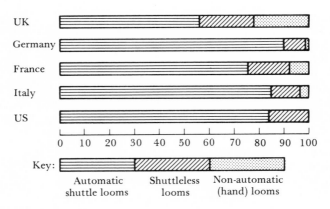

Source: See chart 5.2.
[a]Including non-automatic (hand) looms.

Chart 5.3 *Types of looms installed on 1 January 1980, per cent in all looms[a]*

of shuttleless looms in the total loom park,[5] apart from the most recent
years when investment activity in the United Kingdom has been at a low
ebb. But, apparently, whilst the French dismantled their old non-
automatic looms, the British retained a good many of theirs, with the result
that their share in the United Kingdom remained, by early 1980, at 22 per
cent in contrast with 8 per cent in France.

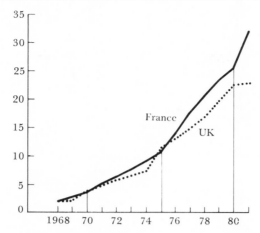

Source: France: Syndicat Général Français de l'Industrie Cotonnière, Paris; UK: Quarterly Statistical Review, Textile Statistics Bureau, Manchester, Nw. 140, Spring 1981.
[a]Including non-automatic looms.

Chart 5.4 *The share of shuttleless looms in total looms installed[a] in France and the United Kingdom, per cent*

Another point thought worth investigating was the mix of raw material consumed in the cotton and allied industries. Again, this does not provide any explanation of the high share of the non-automatic looms in the United Kingdom, where this particular mix was very similar to that of Germany (see chart 5.5) and where the use of non-automatic looms had practically ceased (1 per cent).

The explanation of the problem can probably be found in the views collected in the course of a small-scale enquiry conducted amongst a couple of leading makers of SLs abroad and a handful of British textile manufacturers. In brief, the shuttleless loom is a highly capital-intensive, costly piece of equipment; its advantages are not in doubt but may not everywhere be considered important enough to offset the higher costs. This is particularly important when the industry is in decline and in periods when interest rates are high. Many textile manufacturers are conservative in outlook, especially in the United Kingdom, and find it difficult to justify capital expenditure in view of the depressed state of the industry, cheap imports and poor prospects. All this is more relevant to the British than to many other cotton industries for two reasons. Firstly, its decline started much earlier and secondly, the progression from the non-automatic (Lancashire) to automatic shuttle looms was in any case behind that of other developed countries, because of its historic entrenchment and

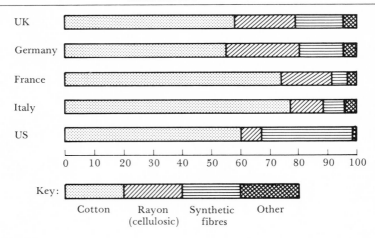

Source: See chart 5.2.

Chart 5.5 *Raw materials consumed by the cotton and allied industries, 1978, per cent in total, by weight*

relatively low labour costs. Thus, Lancashire looms continue to operate where there is a convenient pool of labour, ageing but well trained. In addition, looms last around 80 years and, having been written off in the first twenty years or so, produce without capital cost. All these seemingly apologetic, but justifiable, reasons apply much more to the United Kingdom than to most other countries. Their force is nevertheless reduced when it is considered that in many of those other countries, especially in Europe, the cotton industry was just as established (though perhaps already less out of date) at about the middle of this century, when SLs took off as an innovation. There must have been, therefore, a difference in the attitude to novelties, such as SLs, in the British cotton industry as we have already seen there was in the textile machinery industry.

In many European countries there have been, at various times, government measures aimed at saving the cotton industry. In the United Kingdom the large-scale scrapping of old equipment was subsidised in the later 1950s; this was at a time when SLs were non-existent or in their very early phases and therefore resulted in the replacement of many old Lancashire looms by the modern automatic shuttle looms, with debatable success.[6] Similar help was also given to the cotton industries in other countries. Among more recent examples is Sweden, where most of the big weaveries converted to SLs in the second half of the 1970s by making use of the soft credit offered by the Swedish government for the purchase of modern equipment under a special programme initiated in 1972–3. Thus

Table 5.2 *Loom stocks and cloth production in 1981, percentages in world total*

	Installed weaving machines according to weft insertion system	Cloth production
Conventional looms	85	77
Shuttleless looms	15	23
Of which:		
Rapiers	7	9
Projectiles	4	7
Air jets	2	$3\frac{1}{2}$
Water jets	2	$3\frac{1}{2}$

Source: NIESR Inquiry, one company's estimates.

companies were able to modernise radically without having the necessary cash flow. The case of Sweden is in some way similar to that of Britain. Here, too, a number of older looms survive, primarily in smaller companies where production is specialised and the operating costs of the machines play a relatively smaller role in the price of the product.

Throughout the above discussion of the diffusion of SLs we have used a relatively simple indicator, the number of looms. This is mainly because of the availability of information, or lack of it. However, it should be borne in mind that the capacity of SLs is considerably higher than that of other looms and therefore, if diffusion could be measured by output, SL's shares would be higher. For example, in the Swedish case the share of SLs in production is estimated at about 85 per cent, whilst their share in the number of automatic looms is about 64 per cent and in all looms only 35 per cent.

In table 5.2 we set out the view of one leading textile machinery maker (a company using their own estimates for the world stock of looms in 1981) of the relationship between stocks of looms and production.

The rising share of SLs in the park of the developing countries is certainly worth noting, although some experienced spokesmen of the trade took the view that in the case of at least some of the developing countries it had been a mistake to buy the most modern, sophisticated machinery because the local people were unable to utilise and maintain it properly. This is despite the fact that one of the leading manufacturers who give training with the purchase of their SLs, give longer to teaching operatives from developing countries (a practice probably followed by other machinery makers too). The training takes one to two weeks for operatives from

advanced countries, but three to five weeks for those from less developed
areas but, 'of course', we were told, 'some of the latter cannot write'.

Three further points have been investigated concerning their effect on
the spread of SLs: plant size, energy use and the quality of the yarn.

Projectile or rapier looms can be economically installed in any small
plant and in any number. There are indeed cases of just one or two of them
working efficiently, although naturally not exploiting to the full the
advantages of these machines, since many can be handled by one weaver.
The case of the jet looms is different. Water jets require a fairly complex
water supply system (and equipment for cleaning the polluted water) as
well as a power source for maintaining the permanent pressure of the water
that is more complicated than the power supply of the projectile or rapier
systems and the air jets require the same for air compression. For this
reason, a minimum number of jet looms is needed to make the extra
equipment economically viable, but this is not to say that only the largest
mills can use them.

The question of energy use and the possible effects of higher energy prices
is of secondary importance although the share of energy in total cost of
weaving is considerable (for example, 10 per cent in Germany). Some of
these modern looms, notably the projectiles, required at the time of their
introduction some 30–40 per cent less energy per unit than the conventional automatic shuttle looms. No such saving could be found in the case of
rapiers and the jet looms may require somewhat more energy even than
shuttle looms. With the recently introduced higher speeds, the specific
energy use of all types of SLs has tended to increase somewhat. On the
whole, therefore, it is unlikely that changes in energy prices have
influenced the spread of SLs.

Finally, the quality of yarn should be mentioned, in view of the earlier
fears that the yarn would not be strong enough to meet the higher
requirements of the SLs. This problem has now been overcome: spinners
have started to make stronger yarn, in accordance with the technological
requirements of the more advanced looms.

CONCLUSIONS

The shuttleless loom has been a successful innovation. Most of the new
installations in the advanced countries and a good deal in the less
developed countries have been of this new variety. This will apply even
more in the future and there is still plenty of scope for the further
application of the SLs since, given the very long life of looms of the earlier
types, the share of the new machines in the total loom stock of most
countries' cotton weaving industry is relatively small.

The rate of the further replacement of older looms will depend to a large extent on the state of the textile economy and this will certainly be a deciding factor in the advanced countries. In the less developed areas other considerations may play an important part. In many the labour saving properties of SLs are of little or no significance, for example in India where three quarters of the looms are non-automatic.

For some time to come SLs will retain their position as the leading equipment for modern weaving. They will probably be further developed with the aim of improving their performance and efficiency and possibly also of extending their range to the few varieties of fabrics at present not produced by them. Their position, however, is not entirely unchallenged. The challenge comes partly from other branches of the textile industry, mainly knitting, which has already taken over a part of the earlier market of woven cloth and may further penetrate it, and possibly from non-woven textiles which at the moment do not present any great threat but could be developed further in the more distant future. There are then other possibilities within weaving itself such as the use of circular and multi-phase looms.[7] These are at the moment small in number and probably still at the beginning of their major development phase, but nevertheless considered as one of the possible departures in the future.

The likely long-term trend in some advanced countries is for a whole closed system, from raw material to the finished fabric, with the objectives of high performance, humanisation of the operations and reduction of pollution.[8] Such a system would be totally computerised and SLs could certainly be a part of it. It may seem too 'futurologist' now but it would not be out of line with the development of the cotton textile industry in the past two centuries.

6

FLOAT GLASS

In the 1950s flat glass was made by a number of traditional processes. Depending on the product required, these processes differed mainly by the thickness but also in the quality, chiefly the optical perfection, of the flat glass.

To make polished plate (thicker) glass, molten glass from a furnace was rolled into a continuous ribbon. But because of the glass-to-roller contact, the surfaces became marked and first had to be ground and then polished to produce optically perfect parallel surfaces. The most up-to-date method for this was twin-grinding (grinding the plate on both sides in one operation), evolved in the interwar years by Pilkington in the United Kingdom. By the very nature of the operation, grinding and polishing resulted in glass wastage amounting to some fifth of production, thus involving high capital and operating costs.

Sheet glass (mostly window glass) was made by drawing it vertically in a ribbon from a furnace. This was cheaper than polished plate because it was not ground and polished, but the production method did impart some distortions and it was therefore unacceptable for high quality applications. It was suitable for domestic, horticultural and similar glazing but could not replace polished plate glass.

Three processes, all based on the same fundamental principle, were in use in the early postwar period, one originally developed in Belgium (Fourcault in 1914) and two in the United States (Libbey-Owens in 1915 and Pittsburgh in the early 1920s). It had for a long time been the ambition of glass producers to combine the main features of both processes: to make glass with the relative simplicity and brilliant surfaces of sheet glass but to achieve the parallel surfaces and optical perfection of polished plate. Float glass proved to be the answer.

The 'float' idea was conceived in 1952. The target was to make the high quality glass essential for shop windows, cars, mirrors and other applications where distortion-free glass was necessary, in a way that was more economical than the costly and wasteful grinding and polishing method. It took seven years before the inventor, Sir Alastair Pilkington, and his team were able to bring the flat process to perfection. In the new process a continuous ribbon of glass moves out of the melting furnace and floats along the surface of a bath of molten tin. The ribbon is held at a high enough temperature for a sufficiently long time for the irregularities to melt out and for the surfaces to become flat and absolutely parallel. The ribbon is then cooled down while still on the molten tin until the surfaces are hard enough for it to be taken out of the bath without being marked by the rollers, thus producing a glass of uniform thickness, with brightly polished, optically perfect surfaces, requiring no further treatment, that is, avoiding the grinding and polishing.

In the beginning the float process could successfully produce glass about 6mm ($\frac{1}{4}$ inch) thick. About half of the market for high quality flat glass was for this thickness. The problem then was how to extend the process to produce thicker and thinner glass, since it was obvious that the full potential of float glass could not be realised without mastering the ribbon thickness. The first direction which this expansion took was into the thicker varieties: by the early 1960s further development of the method allowed the making of glass up to 5cm (2 inches). Going downward in thickness required more time but, even before the float process had been further stretched to include the production of thinner window glass as required by the mass market, its advantages were obvious and proven.

Briefly, these advantages were: excellent quality; large scale production, both in terms of the width and length of the plate and also the capacity of the float line; high productivity; and energy saving which, at least in some cases, amounted to 50 per cent in terms of the energy used per unit of final product. There was also a considerable reduction in pollution and an improvement in working conditions by virtue of the smaller number of working places exposed to extreme heat and the elimination of industrial illnesses of the silicosis type which had been difficult to avoid during the grinding and polishing phase of the earlier system.

There were, however, two disadvantages which impeded the rapid diffusion of the process. First, the building of a float line meant heavy investment and secondly, the large capacity of even a relatively small float line, if used efficiently, means that production exceeds the total glass requirements of a smaller country. In other words, the float process required a large market.

The innovator of the float process, Pilkington Brothers in England, acquired a world licence. After the successful application of the invention in their works a spate of manufacturing licences followed in the 1960s. Under these agreements, Pilkington received a disclosure fee, a once-and-for-all payment for each float line put down and a royalty on sales during the life of the licence. An important clause in the agreement concerned improvements in the process; this gave each licensee an incentive to undertake development work. Improvements made by Pilkington went automatically and freely to all licensees but any patented improvement made by any of them could be sold to other licensees (with the exception of Pilkington, who were to receive it free).

The float process did, however, leave certain smaller segments of the flat glass industry untouched. These were: pressed and cast (and often rolled) glass which serve special industrial and ornamental purposes.

The development of the process, with particular relevance to the thickness of glass produced, has been described in some detail in view of the importance of this characteristic. The main development in the past ten to fifteen years has been the extension of the range of the float process into the area of thinner glass, enabling it to make window glass, even though it was originally meant to produce polished plate glass. Thus, at present the lower limit of the thickness of glass produced efficiently by the float process is 1.3mm.

Other areas of product development have also been exploited, such as tinted glass (by firing in ions of copper under the surface of the clear float glass) or the security glass used in automobiles, as well as higher value products that are the result of the combination of glass with other, mainly synthetic, materials. Another development was the modification of the float process in 1975 to produce coloured patterned glass with a smooth surface, competing with traditional patterned glass manufactured by the rolled process.

Electronic control has been applied on a wider front to the whole logistic of the glassmaking process (including the warehousing, where thousands of miles of glass ribbon a year are cut and handled) and particularly to the energy economy of the plants. The latter is important since energy accounts for well over 10 per cent of production costs.

German experience has shown that float lines, in common with every other glassmaking plant, require a major overhaul at intervals of five to six years, in the course of which parts of the productive equipment are almost literally rebuilt. At each of these overhauls an improvement in the specific energy consumption is achieved, resulting in a saving of energy of the order of 10 to 25 per cent by means of better refractories more tailored to the job, improved electronic controls, more efficient insulation and the recycling of waste heat. Better mastery of the method and minor modifications have also contributed to the raising of the capacity of the float line: the original daily capacity of about 400 tonnes has been increased gradually and is estimated nowadays at between 600 and 800 tonnes.

The float process might also have contributed indirectly to the changing market structure of the glass industry. In the earlier study the interconnected nature of European flat glass manufacturing was described as one of the specialities of this industry: 'Apart from Britain, France and Belgium, it is meaningless to speak of 'national' industries in the context of decisions to embark on such a large and indivisible investment as the building of a float plant; such decisions are likely to be taken outside national boundaries'.[1] This situation has in the meantime become even more complex; there may have been many reasons for the change but important contributory factors were certainly the large amount of capital necessary for a float plant and the position of Pilkington, unique in the sense of holding the world licence and with a substantial income from royalties payable under the licence agreements.

The Pilkington Group itself operates nine float plants (four in England, three in Germany, one in Sweden and one in South Africa); it has further interests in float plants in Canada and Mexico and a projected plant in Brazil; it has direct or indirect interests in Australia, Finland and Taiwan as well as a 30 per cent shareholding in Libbey-Owens-Ford, the second largest United States glass company.[2] Among other changes in Europe, the most noteworthy have been the penetration into the small number of European glass producers of one Japanese and two major American companies (the Asahi company in Belgium, Pittsburgh in Italy and France, and Guardian in Luxembourg), further internationalising the European flat glass industry.

THE DIFFUSION OF THE FLOAT PROCESS

Diffusion can be measured in a number of ways. In this particular case the best illustration of the spread of the float glass process is to compare the number of licensed float plants worldwide. Not counting the plants of the world licence holder (Pilkington), this number indicates a spectacular growth: in 1971 there were 29 such plants in operation or under construction in the world; in 1982 this number was 88. Of course, not only the number of plants rose but also that of the licensees and the number of countries where float lines operate, as indicated in chart 6.1.

In the United Kingdom, where Pilkington is the only producer of flat glass and operates four float plants, practically all flat glass that can be made by the float process is manufactured by this method. Only speciality glasses are pressed, cast and/or rolled. More recently, however, the development of the float process has started to make some inroads into that market too, as briefly mentioned in the previous section.

In Germany, the largest producer of glass in Europe, where the number of float lines reached six in 1979 (see chart 6.2), almost 100 per cent of the window glass is float glass, whilst in 1976 one third of production was still accounted for by traditional methods. Probably almost the whole of polished plate glass for which the float method was originally intended is also made by the float system.

In France, the traditional productive equipment has now been totally dismantled and flat glass is being made exclusively by the four float plants

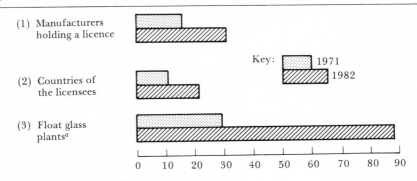

Source: Pilkington Brothers Plc.
*a*Plants in operation, projected or under construction.

Chart 6.1　*Licences of the float glass process, numbers*

operating there, although there remain a number of production units casting and rolling special products.

In Italy, there are five float plants in operation, covering about 70 per cent of total installed capacity; the share of float glass rose from 26 per cent of all flat glass in 1970 to 68 per cent in 1980 (see chart 6.3). Part of the remaining capacity is accounted for by makers of special glass using the casting method, but there are still units applying the earlier, traditional methods in smaller companies for producing flat glass of the 'floatable' varieties.

The float glass story in Sweden is a case of all or nothing, because of the minimum efficiency scale of the only float line, built by Pilkington in the early 1970s. The Scandinavian case deserves some elaboration, however, because it indicates clearly certain general aspects of technological development.

The earlier study (*op.cit.* p.212) reported on what was then the newest flat glass plant in Europe, erected on a greenfield site in Korsør, Denmark, as a joint Danish–Swedish venture. The plant was built and operated on the Pittsburgh principle (the traditional method of drawn glass) for two reasons; first, that the demand for plate glass in the whole of Scandinavia would lag behind the capacity of one single float line; and secondly, that the float process could not then produce thinner sheet glass, for which there was a demand. The first argument was valid, but decisive only if the product range of the float process remained restricted to plate glass. The second argument was an example of technological shortsightedness since soon after the then new plant came on stream the float process was developed further and started to produce thinner sheet glass; thus this argument rapidly became invalid. This brought about marked changes in the Scandinavian glass industry.

a) Number of float glass plants

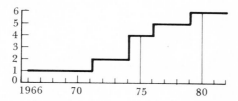

b) The share of float glass in total window glass output, per cent

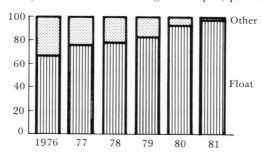

c) Output of window glass, million m²

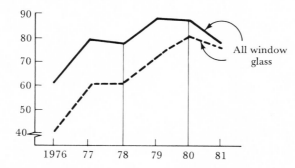

Source: Inquiry, based on national statistics.

Chart 6.2   *The float process in Germany*

In 1976 Pilkington's new float plant started production in Sweden. In 1977 the Norwegian flat glass producer (Drammen) went bankrupt; in 1978 the other Swedish flat glass producer (Emmaboda) stopped producing flat glass; and finally in 1982 the Danish plant at Korsør, built just over a decade earlier, was closed down. In all three cases the chief, though not exclusive, reason was competition from the new float plant which could produce more cheaply. There seems to be no doubt, however, that for any one of the three Scandinavian countries a float plant would be 'too big'.

The shares of float and other flat
glass in total flat glass production, The production of flat glass (all
per cent   types), thousand tonnes

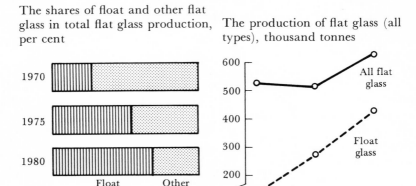

Source: Inquiry, based on national statistics.

Chart 6.3   *The float process in Italy*

There is now only one flat glass producer beside the Pilkington factory left
in the Nordic countries, that in Finland; at the end of the 1970s it was saved
from financial difficulties by the state and Pilkington now has a 50 per cent
share in it. In spite of Pilkington's interest in the firm it has not been
converted to the float process, presumably in view of the small market in
Finland.

The size of the market and the relatively 'excessive' capacity of a float
line is the main reason why an otherwise highly developed industrial
country like Austria still retains a glass industry operating on outdated
technology.

The market size is, in a way, hindering the spread of the float process in
the developing countries. It should be remembered in this context that
while in the industrial countries a crude estimate of *per capita* glass
consumption is about 10–12 kilograms a year, in developing areas it is not
more than 1–1½ kilograms a year. Therefore, the question of market size
in the developing countries has to be approached differently from that
in the advanced countries. This is not to say that there have been no
advances at all in the developing countries: as early as 1968 one float plant
started production in Mexico and similar plants are being erected in Brazil
and Taiwan (both 'newly industrialising' rather than 'less developed'
countries) but the relatively small demand is a definite obstacle to the
further spread of the float process in the less developed countries also.

CONCLUSIONS

The float process revolutionised the technology of making flat glass. Its range has been considerably widened, to the stage where it now covers all varieties of flat glass, with the exception of the very thinnest products (under 1.3mm). It represents, at present, the last word in glassmaking technology and will probably be developed further in a variety of minor ways, such as increasing its efficiency by small modifications and extending its range into more specialised products, those with improved insulating properties or of the kind hitherto made by pressing, casting and rolling for ornamental and specific industrial uses. Another probable development will aim at the further reduction of energy requirements since, even after the very considerable saving that has been made possible by the float process, glassmaking remains one of the most energy hungry industries.

7

NUMERICALLY CONTROLLED MACHINE TOOLS IN METALWORKING

Machine tools (MT) produce certain parts or components of very heterogeneous and often complex final products and operate over the entire field of metalworking. Their control by numerical input (NC) is relatively new but it does not fundamentally alter their prime objective.

Numerical control differs from the technologies studied in the previous chapters. In all the other cases the product of the technology described can be precisely defined. The steel processes produce steel, the tunnel kiln manufactures bricks, the float process makes glass and shuttleless looms make textile fabrics, but the products of machine tools can form a part of very diverse objects, ranging from zip fasteners to aircraft. Accordingly, the diffusion of NCMTs cannot be restricted to specific branches of the metalworking industries and this makes the measurement of the level and speed of the diffusion and, in particular, their international comparison, more difficult.

NC is a system for the automation of variable work phases on metalworking MTs. It is based on the input of numerical (that is, digital) data into the MT, whose action is controlled by the programmed and transmitted instruction, which prescribes all the operations necessary for the execution of the MT's function. The instructions are transmitted onto the information medium (originally a punched tape) and an electronic adapter attached to the MT (the numeric) conveys them as control commands to the machine. Thus, NC is identical to electronic control.

The three basic types of NC are positioning, straight-line cutting and contouring. The first is the simplest. The MT is adjusted to a certain position and processes the metal. In straight-line cutting the MT will do any operation on the workpiece as long as it is moved in a straight line between two points of reference. Contouring controls shape the workpiece in any direction, in lines and curvatures of two or three dimensions. The first type is applied mainly to the simpler drilling and punching machines, the second to relatively uncomplicated milling and lathe work, and contouring for practically anything.

The idea of NCMTs was probably triggered off by the electronic fire-control developed in the United States for air defence during the war.[1] The first step was a programme consisting of a series of holes punched in a tape, controlling the operating sequence. From this small beginning, the idea was developed until it reached the complex performance of contouring controls.

Because the development was gradual it is difficult to draw dividing lines and tie them to definite dates. The direction, however, is clearly from the inflexible to more flexible types of control. At first, once the programmes were punched they and the tools were hard to change. Now the machining centres, introduced in the 1960s, change their tools automatically and carry out many machining operations. Also since the 1960s, instructions can be fed into the MT by a computer mounted on the machine itself, consisting of microprocessors and memory, making it possible to enter new data and enable the MT to be programmed to make a range of products (computer numerical control CNC).

The next step, in line with the development of microelectronics and computer technology, was to link NCMTs to central computers controlling their whole production run. This system, direct numerical control (DNC), enables the operator to obtain information on the objects being machined, often simultaneously, on the various MTs linked to the computer, checking the work in progress, which could also be done by many CNCs but only on one MT.

The different degrees of sophistication are, of course, reflected in the price of these machines or machine-systems. The price range of NCMTs has important implications for their diffusion and therefore it is worth noting, as a very crude illustration, that whereas a simple NC lathe may cost about £10,000–£15,000 today, a CNC machine would be from £50,000 upwards; the simplest of the versatile machine centres probably starts at £150,000, and the complex varieties can reach £1 million or more.

In view of the great price difference between conventional and NC machine tools it is worth asking whether NCMTs pay off, and if so, over what period? Because of the difference that often occurs between the *ex ante* calculated pay off period (in whatever way calculated) and the actual *ex post* result, it is important to quote only from actual experience. This, however, is difficult to come by. When asked, NC users, almost without exception, emphasised the economic, as distinct from the technical, efficiency of NCMTs but were reluctant to quantify them on the grounds that much depends on the degree of utilisation of the expensive high-technology machines and on the complexity of the operation. These differ not only from machine to machine but also from operation to operation. Whilst stressing the importance of these factors, a major German report[2] contains a few actual figures that are reported in graphical form in chart 7.1. (The lines on the chart are purely hypothetical since the small number

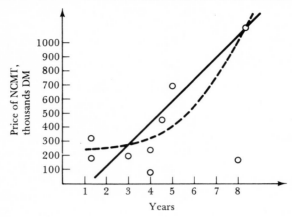

Source: See note 2.

Note: The observations (o) are real, the lines (⁓⁓⁓) are hypothetical.

Chart 7.1 *Pay-off period of NCMTs (years of amortisation)*

of observations does not make any more concrete estimates possible.) It appears that in seven of the nine cases the pay off period was less than five years. In some cases the pay off period is surprisingly long, but of course there may have been special reasons (for example, to overcome extreme complexity) for installing NCMTs.

The most recent development links a set of machining centres so that parts processed by each of them can travel amongst the centres in different pre-set sequences under computer control. Also under the same control are automatic conveyors for palletised transportation, usually with robotic manipulation. This system can make a wide range of parts or components of the same family and needs little attention once the system has been adequately programmed. Such a system costs several million pounds. There are only a few of these flexible, computer-controlled manufacturing systems in operation as yet. Japan, the United States and Germany lead the way and in other countries there are either just a few of them in use or none at all.[3]

At the time of our previous study NC was still in its infancy, struggling with teething troubles, although its dissemination through industry had already started. The technique has changed and developed considerably during the 1970s. Among the most noteworthy developments are the widespread application of mini-computers, that is CNC; automatic tool change; manual data input; better tape proving techniques; and the advance made towards the flexible manufacturing system described above. Apart from the controls, other advances have also been achieved, such as improved cutting tools and the replacement of hydraulic servo-drives with DC motors.

NCMTs have also become bigger and can manage more complicated tooling. Very generally speaking, an NCMT of the 1980 type, according to American calculations, has more than three times the capacity of the NCMT of 1970. With increased reliability and performance, idle machine time during the workshift has been reduced; utilisation has also risen by linking NCMT to other machines in the production system. The automatic tool changer was a big step towards the fuller utilisation of the capacity of NCMTs and it also enabled one operator to supervise several machines. The equipment around the NCMT has increased in importance and sophistication. Automatic measuring devices control the wear of tools and test the quality of the product (although generally, except for the most expensive, modern types, only when the NCMT is not operating; in-process inspection is not yet widespread); handling devices automatically feed in details, and so on.

The nature of NC operations has also changed. Earlier NCMTs served mainly metalcutting operations and although this has remained the function of the bulk of NCMTs, NC has been used increasingly for other metalworking operations as well, such as metalforming (pressing, bending) and welding.

Among the most recent departures of the research and development programme covering NC, the most important is probably the fuller computerisation of programming. To a small extent this has already been implemented but considerable further development is needed in order to extend it over a wider area. Parallel with increased sophistication there is also a move towards simpler and cheaper control systems. This would make NC applicable to more machines and further reduce the cost of NCMT to a level which small firms could afford. There are quite a number of functions on a sophisticated machine that CNC can do and whose disse-mination across industry is just a question of time, such as the registration by internal clock of operating time in various ways (per batch, per piece, per tool, and so on), viewing screens for immediate optical information and fault detection.

All these changes and other minor ones have greatly widened the range of economic viability of NCMTs. Some ten to fifteen years ago the area of economic application of NCMTs was still fairly sharply delineated into small and medium-sized batches. There were exceptions, for example highly complex operations on one-off pieces but, in general, NCMTs were not used in the production of workpieces in numbers above or below certain limits. The range most favourable to NC machining was within five to fifty pieces. (Technically, of course, NCMTs could handle any number, one or a million, but their input was less economically viable than traditionally controlled MTs for very small numbers, or semi- and fully-automatic machines for higher ones.)

Chart 7.2 indicates fairly simply, on the basis of research conducted in

A: increasing repetition, rising batch size, reducing number of programmes needed.
B: increasing complexity of the workpiece.

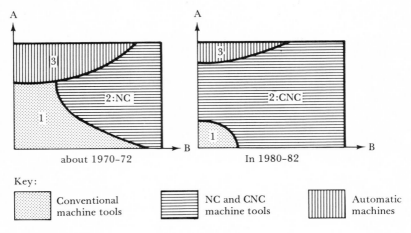

about 1970–72   In 1980–82

Key:

Conventional machine tools	NC and CNC machine tools	Automatic machines

Source: See note 2.

Chart 7.2 *The increasing scope of NCMTs*

Germany, how computerisation extended the area of viable and efficient input of NCMTs. (This, however, cannot be projected into the future. On the one hand, certain workpieces will probably always be made by traditional, non-NC, machines and, on the other, the development of robotics will influence the application of NCMTs in higher-volume operations.)

Our recent survey among a random (and statistically unrepresentative) selection of NC users in the United Kingdom also indicates that the demarcation lines are now much less sharp and that NCMTs have come to be applied more widely. Some even take the view that neither batch size nor complexity is a factor which limits the use of NCMTs. The general view is nevertheless more conservative and tends to indicate that NCMTs are not used for working pieces of low complexity and hence low value, nor are they used for high volume production which remains the realm of specialised automatic machines. The same survey provides the basis of the view that a much higher part of production could be performed efficiently by NCMTs than is the case now. This latter statement is not based only on technicalities; it can be supported by economic considerations too. First, in view of the technological development, the cost per function of NCMTs has decreased very markedly; this extends the range of economically efficient NC applications and, moreover, new functions can be built in at low cost. Secondly, although NCMTs are naturally more expensive than traditional (non-NC) machines, the price difference has narrowed considerably. Indeed, in recent years, the price of NCMTs actually fell owing to larger production, reduced costs of microelectronic controls and so on. The figures shown in table 7.1 indicate the development of machine tool prices in the United Kingdom. Price indices in other countries are likely to show different movements since these prices are influenced by exchange rate developments (because of the high share of imported NCMTs), but the general trend is doubtless very similar.

Table 7.1. *Price indices of machine tools in the United Kingdom (1975 = 100)*

	1980	1981	1982
Metal-cutting MTs			
all types	214	231	249
all NC types	161	147	155
multi-function NCMTs	168	132	132

Source: *Business Monitors* (PA 332), HMSO, London.

THE DIFFUSION OF NCMTS

From various sources and from our inquiry the diffusion of NCMTs has been investigated on two levels: the production of NCMTs and the use (that is, the stock) of these new machines, in other words the NC technology.

It is convenient to start with an illustration of the pattern of world production and exports of machine tools (see table 7.2). In 1981, the world's largest producer of machine tools was the United States, followed very closely by Japan; Germany was not far behind, producing (in value terms) as much as the four next largest producers (Italy, the United Kingdom, France and Switzerland) taken together. Germany, however, was well ahead of any other country as an exporter, whilst Switzerland exported the largest part of her production.

It is reasonable to assume that most of the world production of NCMTs originates in those countries that are the leaders in machine tool production. Thus the study of the diffusion of this technology has been limited to the European countries mentioned above, that is Germany, France, Italy and the United Kingdom, and to the United States and Japan. We were not in a position to cover Switzerland but have included Sweden, another country with a highly developed machine tool industry. Whilst not every method of measuring diffusion could be applied to each

Table 7.2. *World machine tool production and
exports, 1981, per cent share in total*

	Production (A)	Exports (B)	B:A (C)
US	19.5	11.1	0.6
Japan	18.4	16.4	0.9
West Germany	15.3	24.2	1.6
USSR	12.2	3.1	0.3
Italy	5.3	6.8	1.3
UK	3.5	4.7	1.3
France	3.1	3.8	1.2
Switzerland	3.1	7.0	2.3
E Germany	2.9	5.3	1.8
Others	16.7	17.6[a]	1.1

[a]Of which: Czechoslovakia 3.1 per cent.
Source: *Machine tool statistics*, Machine Tool Trades Association,
London (based on American Machinist), 1982.

country, the picture which emerges seems sufficiently well supported by statistical evidence.

The production of NCMTs (see table 7.3) has increased sharply in the second half of the 1970s. The table shows clearly the leading role of Japan where, having overtaken the United States in 1977, by 1979 NCMT production was already almost twice the United States output in the same year. Germany's NCMT production rose the fastest: it increased almost fivefold in the five years to 1981. As compared to most other countries shown, the United Kingdom's performance has been lagging behind: British NCMT production (by number) was one fifth of the German and less than one half of the Italian output in 1981.

Whilst table 7.3 demonstrates the upswing in the production of NCMTs in numbers, in two respects it is not the whole story. First, the value of various NCMTs differs greatly depending on the complexity of the machine and second, it does not show the relative importance of NCMTs in the machine tool industry as a whole. From these points of view the share of the value of NCMTs in total MT production may be a more useful indicator. This is shown for the same countries (except France) and also for Sweden in chart 7.3.

In chart 7.3 the United Kingdom position is somewhat better because the lower number of NCMTs represents a percentage share in the similarly lower total output which is, although the smallest among the countries included, not very far behind that of Germany. The Japanese leadership,

Table 7.3 *Production of NCMTs, numbers*

	US[a]	Japan	France	Germany	Italy	UK
1972	1,630	. .	. .	622	360	381
1973	2,865	2,765	. .	808	513	462
1974	4,210	3,040	535	985	598	709
1975	4,136	2,182	612	1,085	759	739
1976	3,856	3,286	576	1,289	783	612
1977	4,482	5,436	574	1,979	1,013	724
1978	5,688	7,336	867	2,451	1,448	969
1979	7,178	13,514	1,068	3,258	2,124	1,058
1980	8,856	. .	. .	4,743	2,662	1,240
1981	. .	. .	. .	5,672	2,459	1,084

Source: VDMA Fachgemeinschaft Werkzeugmaschinen, Frankfurt; *Statistisches Jahrbuch*, Wiesbaden; *Economic Handbook of the Machine Tool Industry*, National Machine Tool Builders Association, McLean, Va, USA; ISCO, Rome; *OECD Observer* No. 115, March 1982; *Business Monitors* (UK), various issues.
[a]Metalcutting MTs only.

however, remains clear: half of their MT production consisted of NCMTs in 1980. Noteworthy too is the relatively high NC share of Sweden and, to a lesser degree, also that of Italy.

Whilst the NC technique was initially developed and innovated in the United States, towards the end of the 1970s the Japanese took over the leadership and became the trendsetters. A good deal of this is no doubt due to their leading position in microelectronics. Characteristic of the leading role of the Japanese producers is the fact that about half of the recent NCMT imports of Germany (otherwise the leading exporter of machine tools) originated in Japan. However, the Japanese conditions being specific and unique, chart 7.4 illustrates some notable trends in NCMT production using the example of Germany, whose industrial experience seems more relevant to European conditions.

Although the indicators shown in this chart have been specially assembled from German sources and reflect the trends in the German industry, they can be taken as fairly representative of the situation in other countries whose industries, to a greater or lesser extent, share the German experience. The main messages of chart 7.4 are as follows. Firstly, the number of NCMT producers more than doubled in ten years to 1981; the controls themselves are produced by considerably fewer firms and their number rose only slowly. (In most countries except Japan many of the controls are imported, mainly from Japan.) Secondly, the average weight of NCMTs has come down following the general trend towards lighter

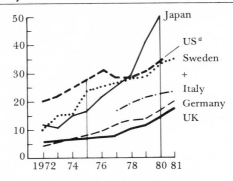

Source: As table 7.3 and IUI, Sweden.
[a]Metalcutting MTs only; on the same basis the figures for Germany and the United Kingdom would be about 27 per cent, as marked by +.

Chart 7.3   *The share of NCMTs in the total production of MTs, per cent*

equipment which, in this case, went hand in hand with rapidly rising sophistication, contributing markedly to the rise in the average price per kilogram. The average price per kilogram is sometimes used to assess the technological status of engineering products: the higher the price, the more advanced the product. Thirdly, the average value of the controls has decreased gradually (in real terms more sharply than shown on the chart) reflecting the fall in the costs of microelectronics; the share of the value of the controls in the total value of the NCMTs fell even more sharply however; it halved in the ten years to 1981. Lastly, CNC began to be applied to MTs in Germany in 1977 and by 1981 all but 6 per cent of the NCMTs incorporated computerised (CNC) controls; in five years the number of CNCMTs rose more than eightfold. Production shifted towards the most complex type of NCMTs: contouring NCs accounted for 48 per cent of all controls on German-made NCMTs in 1970 and for 82 per cent in 1979–81; the share of simpler, positioning and straight-line, NCs was correspondingly reduced.

The *production* of NCMTs and their diffusion may be taken as characterising, at least to some extent, the advanced nature and innovative spirit of the machine tool industry in the countries examined. This, however, is no more than a relatively small, though important, segment of the metalworking industry. Another approach to the diffusion of the NC technique is to assess its spread, that is, the degree and speed of its *adoption*, within the much wider category of engineering. For any such assessment either a reliable estimate or a proper census of the machine tools installed in or operated by, the metalworking industry is required and this is a major exercise. The information available is presented in table 7.4 and chart 7.5,

Number of producers

A = Average weight (tonnes/NCMT)
B = Average price per kg (DM/kg)

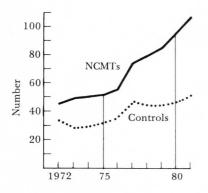

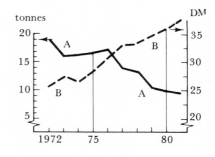

C = Percentage share of the value of controls in the total value of NCMTs
D = Average value of controls (DMooo/piece)

E = Percentage share of CNC in total NCMTs (by number)
F = Number of CNCMTs produced

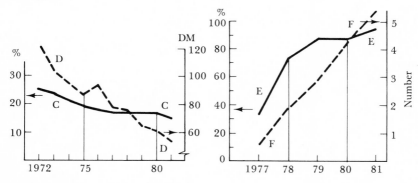

Source: VDMA Fachgemeinschaft Werkzeugmaschinen.

Chart 7.4   *Selected indicators of German NCMT production*

the first showing the stock of NCMTs and the second their share in the total machine tool park. Unfortunately, the latest information for both the United States and Japan relates to 1976.

   The United States started with a very strong lead. In 1969–70 about 20,000 NCMTs were already in operation there; at the same time the number of these machines in the United Kingdom was about 3,000 and in Germany 2,000. In the other European countries they numbered under 1,000 (see note 1 to this chapter). By 1976 the United States park of NCMTs had doubled to 40,000; the second highest stock was in Japan,

Table 7.4 *The stock of NCMTs, thousands*

	Germany	UK	Sweden	Italy	France	US	Japan	USSR
1969–70	1.9	3.2	0.5	0.8	..	20.0	..	..
1973	—	..	1.1		..	29.4	..	11.0
1974	..	..	..		2.6	..	10.5	..
1975	..	..	..	3.3	..	..	..	..
1976	8.0	9.7	2.1		4.0	40.0	14.0	..
1979	..	..	3.7		..	..	..	
1980	25.0	..	4.0		..	..		
1981	..	25.8ᵃ	..	11.4	16.4	..		

Source: See table 7.3; and Diffusione del controllo numerico in Italia, UCIMO, *Censimento* 1981.
[a]1982

followed by the United Kingdom, Germany, France, Italy and Sweden. By 1980, that is, in four years, the German NCMT stock had more than trebled to 25,000, the Swedish doubled, the French rose fourfold from 1976 to 1981, the Italian increased by a factor of $3\frac{1}{2}$ from 1975 to 1981 and the British stock rose from about 10,000 in 1976 to almost 26,000 by 1982. Both the Japanese and the United States park must have risen very markedly; the former may be very crudely estimated as between 35,000 and 40,000 and the latter as around 70,000.

More meaningful than the numbers of NCMTs is their share in the total national machine tool park[4] (see chart 7.5). Although not shown because of lack of information, Japan is probably the leader in this particular league. In 1980, 2.2 per cent of all German machine tools were numerically controlled, a figure reached by Italy one year later, with France marginally behind. In the United Kingdom the share of NCs in the total stock reached 2.6 per cent by 1982. The United States indicator may also be at about this level and is unlikely to be much further ahead. The highest diffusion of NC in the national park, with the exception of Japan, is estimated to have been achieved by Sweden. (Another country where this kind of diffusion might have reached a level comparable to that in Sweden is Switzerland, whose data are unfortunately not known.)

In every country certain categories of users pioneered the application of NC. These were the innovators, others followed them. In Germany in 1969, NCMTs were predominantly used in mechanical engineering; the same industry was the leader in France whilst in the United Kingdom it was joined by the aerospace industry. In Sweden, however, most NCMTs were used in electrical engineering. In each of these countries the importance of the sector which originally led as a user of NCs diminished markedly in the following ten years or so (see chart 7.6) and NC spread faster in other branches of the metalworking industries.

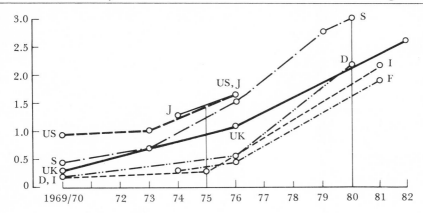

Source: See table 7.3 and author's estimates
Note: US 1976 is for 1976–8. *Definition and coverage varies by country; adopting some other countries' practice the UK share in 1982 works out as 3.3%.*
Country codes: S – Sweden, D – Germany, F – France, I – Italy, J – Japan.

Chart 7.5 *The share of NCMTs in the total MT park, per cent*

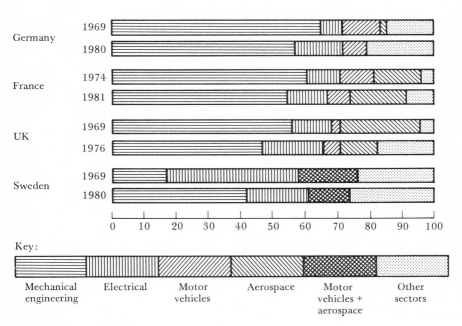

Source: As for 7.3 and note 1.

Chart 7.6 *The distribution of the NC stock by sector, per cent*

We may now ask why diffusion has been relatively slow? After over twenty years still no more than a small percentage of machine tools is numerically controlled. The answer must be approached from various angles. First, one NCMT if properly utilised can easily do the work of several traditional MTs; moreover, one machine centre with NC can replace several individual NCMTs (and of course even more traditional machines). Secondly, replacement should in many cases not be taken literally: unless the floor space is needed for other purposes, the old machine is often retained as a reserve or for occasional work which it can perform cheaply because usually it has been written off. It is thus reasonable to expect that if diffusion could be measured by the value or volume of output, the share of NCMTs would be very significantly higher.

In the course of the random survey of NCMT users in the United Kingdom referred to above some of the respondents were full of praise for NCMTs, although even they added some critical remarks; others, however, were much less enthusiastic. Thus, whilst it was generally admitted that NC machines have many advantages such as efficiency, cost saving, easier planning/scheduling, accuracy and high quality, flexibility, versatility, consistency and floor space saving, some emphasised that while this may be the situation *now*, the reliability of NC machines was much less satisfactory five or more years ago. There were serious troubles in earlier times (one large company added: 'until the Japanese started to produce reliable NCs') and these initial difficulties might have hampered the dissemination of the technique. The relatively high cost as compared with conventional machines has been almost universally mentioned as an obstacle which becomes significant in cases when investment appraisal methods are conservative or even archaic. Others mentioned that in order to realise the full advantage of NC the whole production system might have to be altered. The NC system requires new and often scarce skills, making some of the older craftsmen redundant and this has led to cases of shopfloor opposition and examples of restrictive practices, but there have also been hints of management prejudice against radical change.

What makes all these comments believable is the fact that they come from companies actually using NC, some of them in large numbers. One of them, although mentioning the rapid obsolescence of the control systems as a definite disadvantage, nevertheless admitted that in some cases metal processors could not exist without NC since the manual production of highly complex components is no longer viable.

The respondents in this British survey were almost unanimous in reporting considerable productivity gains; this view is supported by a thorough German study carried out by the Fraunhofer-Institut (see note 2 to this chapter) according to which 'the installation of about 12,000 CNCMTs in the five to seven years to mid-1980 freed about 22,000 workers'. The report also found that CNC has brought about the real breakthrough of NCMTs in the German metalworking industry during the second half of the 1970s. Chart 7.4 provides ample evidence to support this statement. The same report contains information on the batch sizes machined on CNCMTs: 49 per cent of the work performance of the sampled (1,151) CNCMTs consisted of small batches (up to 50), 10 per cent of the production concerned one-off pieces, and 41 per cent batches of more than 50; this again supports the view of the expanding range of NC application.

In the course of the German inquiry, 155 firms reported on the economic effects of CNCMTs; 121 firms considered the economic (cost-effective) advantages the most important, achieved by the reduction of machining time and better utilisation of the machines, that is less downtime; 70 firms mentioned higher flexibility as a noteworthy advantage and 60 firms the improved quality of the product. Other factors were also mentioned, but only by less than 20 or so firms.

These views from both the German and the British industry, the speed of diffusion in recent years and the still relatively low share of NCMTs in the total national machine tool park point to the continued rapid, and possibly accelerating, dissemination of the NC technique in the near future. However, their relatively high price, the scarcity of personnel educated and trained to handle the increasingly complicated machinery and ancillary equipment and the conservatism of both management and workforce all appear to be factors hindering diffusion. They are not easy to overcome but appropriate training schemes, improved information and, last but not least, government support especially geared to the particular properties of the NC technique may help.

Another factor that may have implications for the future of NCMTs is the emergence in the last five to ten years of industrial *robotics*. Robots[5] are, naturally, also numerically controlled and in common with NC they can perform a wide number of functions in various fields; metalworking is only one of them.

ROBOTS

The market for robots has been growing very rapidly, from almost nil in 1975 to US $358 million in 1980 in Japan and the United States alone, as estimated by the OECD. The estimated world population of robots was about 28,400 in 1982 (not counting the centrally planned economies). As the figures in table 7.5 indicate, almost one half of this world population was operating in Japan where there were twice as many robots as in the United States (although some of the Japanese ones might have been of the simpler type). As related to size or population, Sweden is at the head of this league.

Table 7.5. *The world robot population in 1982*

Japan	13,000
US	6,250
W Germany	3,500
Sweden	1,300
UK	1,150
France	950
Italy	700
Belgium	350
Other Western countries	1,200

Source: British Robot Association.

Although the number of robots installed in the United Kingdom is relatively small it is of some interest to note that of the 1,150 robots installed at the end of 1982 only about 25 per cent were British made (or assembled), 24 per cent were supplied by the United States, 14 per cent by Japan and the remaining 37 per cent by various European manufacturers.

A certain amount of overlap between robots and NCMTs is unavoidable; its extent was the subject of a Swedish investigation conducted in 1979 by the Government Committee of Computers and Electronics (DEK) covering 47 NCMT and 43 robot installations. The main findings of this wide-ranging inquiry can be summed up as follows. First, there is a clear tendency for NCMTs to be used in smaller and medium-sized series and robots in long series. Second, NCMTs tend to have longer periods of operation than robots. Third, the number of variations (of detail) on the workpiece is higher (ten and more) in the case of NCMTs than robots, which are characterised predominantly by a small number of variations (typically one to five). Fourth, re-tooling is much simpler for NCMTs; half of the robots in the sample were re-tooled once a week and there were none with more than ten re-toolings, whereas no more than 9 per cent of the NCMTs were re-tooled once only, 70 per cent between two to ten times and 21 per cent more than ten times. Lastly, for two thirds of the robots the average batch size was more than 1,000, whilst 93 per cent of the batch sizes on NCMTs were under 1,000 and 53 per cent under 100.

To sum up, the typical NCMT in this inquiry was operating in a plant producing less than 10,000 units a year; the average working time exceeded five minutes per workpiece and a relatively large number of variations was performed on them; the NCMT was re-tooled two to ten times a week, thus the average batch size was less than 100 units on average. All the indicators for the robots covered in the inquiry showed almost exactly the opposite. It follows that, apart from the unavoidable grey areas of overlap, robots will not markedly affect the further application of NCMTs; indeed, it seems more likely that the spread of robots, which has been rapid in recent years, will make the installation of NCMTs more desirable and in many cases inescapable.

CONCLUSIONS

The technique of numerical control as applied to metalworking machine tools has developed very significantly in the past ten to fifteen years. NCMTs have become more complex, performing their tasks more reliably and efficiently over a widening range of products. Although an increasing proportion of machine tools have been equipped with numerical control (probably more than half in the case of Japan, the leading NCMT producer) no more than a relatively small percentage of the national machine tool park is accounted for by NCMTs (even though the NC share in output is probably much higher). Despite weighty hindering factors, such as relatively high investment cost, scarcity of special skills and conservatism, the further speedy diffusion of the NC technique seems more than probable.

The future development is likely to be in the direction of new automated unmanned features on the machines themselves, their integration into gradually widening flexible computer-aided manufacture which will include automatic loading, transfer and inspection, probably in parallel with and perhaps even promoted by industrial robots. There are already a number of examples where such complex applications are being pioneered and their further extensive development is almost a certainty.

8

CONCLUSIONS

The objectives of this study were set out in the introduction. Briefly, the intention was to measure the diffusion of the selected processes, their development since about 1970, the reasons for the survival of the earlier technologies where applicable, any particular factors promoting or hindering diffusion, the outlook for the future of the processes and the effect on diffusion of three particular aspects, size, the energy situation and the role of governments. In many respects these objectives are linked. In the summary that follows they will be dealt with on the basis of the preceding case study chapters, supplemented by other relevant observations.

DIFFUSION

Measuring the diffusion was relatively easy in some of the six cases and very difficult in others; the availability of statistical information has varied a great deal. As a consequence, no uniformity of measurement was possible but it is believed that the indicators chosen give a sufficiently good idea of the speed and degree of dissemination of the processes which had been new in the 1960s but which had reached different degrees of maturity during the period of this investigation.

The previous six chapters include many details on the diffusion of the processes; a brief description of the situation will therefore suffice here.

The *basic oxygen steelmaking* process has almost completely ousted the earlier (open hearth and Thomas) technologies in the course of the last ten to twelve years and, together with the electric furnace, has become *the* major process for steelmaking. In this sense it has reached saturation in most advanced countries. The other major technology in the steel industry, *continuous casting*, still lags behind in the diffusion process. Because of earlier unsolved operational problems its dissemination has been slower than that of BOP but it is an essential part of the modern steelmaking process and its further rapid application is likely. The *tunnel kiln* is approaching saturation point in the brick industries of many, though not all, countries. Most of the new looms installed recently in the cotton and allied weaving industries of the advanced countries were of the *shuttleless* variety (and to a lesser extent the same applies to some of the less developed countries) but so far they have replaced only a part of the older type looms and there is obviously a long way to go before even half of the loom stock is shuttleless. The *float* process is now the universally accepted technology for manufacturing flat glass in all advanced countries where the market size is big enough to accommodate the output of a float line. Despite considerable technical development, *numerically controlled machine tools* still account for no more than a very small percentage of the machine tool park of even the most advanced countries, or for a rising minority share of their production of machine tools.

Before going any further in discussing diffusion, it should be remembered that the period under investigation in this book, that is, from 1970 onwards, differs greatly from that of the earlier study.[1] The years since 1970 have been dominated by two oil shocks. The first, in 1973–4, was followed in 1975 by the deepest recession since the war, from which there was only moderate recovery and which led into years of stagnation or very slow growth in the world economy. Although there had been recessions in the 1950s and 1960s as well, they were milder and shorter and were followed by rapid recovery. The past ten years, however, have been in sharp contrast to the *belle époque* of the two postwar decades.

The introduction of major innovations is, to a large degree, the function of investment. Whilst in the 1960s gross fixed investment in the OECD countries rose on average by about $6\frac{1}{2}$ per cent a year in real terms, this growth rate sank to about $1\frac{1}{3}$ per cent a year in the 1970s. Investment in manufacturing, which is more relevant to the adoption of new industrial processes, has experienced the same or a bigger proportional decline and in a number of countries or years it actually fell.

Thus, the general economic climate was unfavourable to investment, a necessary requisite for the diffusion of relatively new production methods. Yet our diffusion curves do not provide evidence of a slowing down in the speed of diffusion. This is in spite of the fact that none of the industries that are the chief users of these technologies were exceptionally fortunate in escaping the general economic malaise. The six technologies affect five major industrial sectors. Three of them, steel, bricks and glass, produce basic materials while two, textiles and engineering, are in different categories. The steel industries of the advanced countries have experienced great trouble in the past ten years; the brick and glass industries were also deeply affected by the slump, which was almost general in the construction industries of the advanced countries. Demand for textiles has been better maintained but the industries of the advanced countries have declined as a result of sharp competition from LDC producers and the outcome of worldwide structural changes. Finally, the generally unfavourable conditions have left their mark on the metalworking/engineering industries as well. Thus, the difference in the fortunes of these industries is not very marked although the basic industries probably fared worse than the processing sectors such as textiles or engineering.

The advance of the new technologies has nevertheless been maintained.

This can be explained in two ways. The first involves the pressure of competition. In times of slack demand competition becomes keener and those who already have the advantage of the reduction in costs resulting from the installation of the most up-to-date technology leave all the others handicapped. The incentive to imitate them by innovating is strong, stronger than in boom years. At the same time, however, many industries and, to an even greater extent, many individual companies, are forced to contract because of falling or stagnating demand and the emergence of new producers elsewhere. This is the second factor which results in wholesale scrapping of productive facilities. It is natural that the oldest plants operating the earlier, more expensive technology will be closed down. Rapid diffusion can be the result of the growth of best practice techniques as defined by Salter,[2] or the amputation of a part of the tail of the Salter structure: the oldest, least productive equipment or, as is usually the case, a combination of both.

In the period under consideration there have been many examples of the adoption of best practice techniques, but also those of scrapping older equipment and indeed there is evidence that the latter has been proceeeding at an extraordinary rate, often resulting in an absolute decline of total national (or company) capacity.

In the United Kingdom, a sharp reduction of about 50 per cent in steel capacity became official policy in recent years; the capacity of the Swedish steel industry was reduced by one fifth from 1975 to 1981; and in Germany the share of BOP grew in the 1970s as a consequence of the dismantling of open hearth and Thomas plants rather than through the expansion of BOP.

The number of brick kilns was greatly reduced in Germany, France and the United Kingdom in the course of the 1970s. In Sweden, the diffusion process of the tunnel kilns consisted exclusively of scrapping, not only the older Hoffmann type kilns, but also some relatively new tunnel kilns. In the glass industry, the float system made all the other plants redundant in the countries where it was introduced. The example of the closure of the Danish plant was described in some detail in chapter 6.

The number of machine tools in Germany was reduced by 10 per cent between 1976 and 1980. This equals about 125,000 machines.[3] In the same period the number of NCMTs rose by about 17,000. For there to be no change in capacity, each NCMT would need the capacity of more than seven other machines. This seems impossible, so there must have been a considerable reduction in capacity. In the United States the situation is similar. The machine tool stock fell by 14 per cent from 1973 to 1978; again for there to be no change in capacity this would imply a replacement ratio of more than twenty; an equally impossible figure. In the small British sample survey mentioned in chapter 7 we received the data set out in table

Table 8.1. *Machine tool stock in the British*
sample companies, 1970 = 100

	1970	1975	1982
All machine tools	100	101	90
NC machine tools	100	138	198
Share of NCMTs, per cent	*1.7*	*2.3*	*3.7*

Source: Inquiry.

8.1. The result of this small-scale survey supports the nationwide German and American experience. The fall in the machine tool park only began after 1975 and in that period the replacement ratio works out at eleven, again an impossibly high figure, indicating a significant reduction in capacity, at least in these terms.

The best illustration, however, can be found in the cotton weaving industry (see table 8.2). The contraction in this industry was very marked in both France and the United Kingdom. From 1968 to 1981 the number of looms was reduced by more than a third in the former and two thirds in the latter. The share of shuttleless looms increased considerably in both countries, yet this increase owed much more to the large-scale scrapping of old looms than to the installation of new SLs. In the British case, the number of SLs rose from 1,200 in 1968 to 5,500 in 1981 or by 4,300, but in the same period the total number of looms fell by 66,000. In the French case the SL stock rose by 7,600 but the total number of looms was 37,000 lower at the end of the same period than at its beginning.

The head and tail of the Salter structure described above can thus be demonstrated empirically. In the case of shuttleless looms the rapid diffusion was largely the consequence of cutting off the tail, that is, scrapping old capacity. In view of the unfavourable economic conditions and the resultant scrapping of older capacity, the diffusion curves rose faster than they otherwise would have done. Although the improvement was real, in a sense it was arithmetic and optical.

For further analysis of the diffusion process, selected indicators have been collected partly from chapters 2 to 7 and partly from earlier work. Where data were available, these indicate for each of the five European countries, Germany, France, Italy, Sweden and the United Kingdom and also for the United States and Japan, the time lag of introduction after the introduction by the country which pioneered the process, the number of years that was necessary for each technology to reach a certain level of diffusion and the most recent diffusion indicator (see table 8.3).

We also repeat the diffusion curves but in a simplified form. The data are

Table 8.2. *Number of looms in the cotton and allied industries, thousands*

	1968	1972	1977	1981	Change 1968–81	
					000	Per cent
United Kingdom						
Shuttleless	1.2	3.6	6.7	5.5	+ 4.3	+ 258
Other automatic	40.6	30.4	24.6	13.2	− 27.4	− 67
Other	48.3	25.2	12.5	5.3	− 43.0	− 89
Total	90.1	59.2	43.8	24.0	− 66.1	− 73
SL share, per cent	*1.3*	*6.1*	*15.3*	*22.9*	. .	. .
France						
Shuttleless	1.3	3.1	6.7	8.9	+ 7.6	+ 485
All other	61.7	45.8	30.7	17.0	− 44.7	− 72
Total	63.0	48.9	37.4	25.9	− 37.1	− 59
SL share, per cent	*2.1*	*6.3*	*17.9*	*34.4*	. .	. .

Source: *Quarterly Statistical Review*, Textile Statistics Bureau, Manchester; Syndicat Général Français de l'Industrie Cotonnière, Paris.

shown at five-yearly intervals for the United Kingdom and Germany and, exceptionally, for other countries (see chart 8.1). Furthermore, we pooled the data in table 8.3 in order to measure the average time lag of introduction, or the number of years required to reach a certain degree of diffusion. The results are shown in table 8.4 and depicted in chart 8.2.

The first objective of this analysis was to check the validity of the belief that the diffusion in this particular representation follows the form of an S-curve. The figures do not provide much concrete evidence for the exclusive validity of any very regular S-curve but they definitely support the rational expectation of some kind of an S-curve. This question has been the subject of considerable speculation in economic literature[4] and therefore our finding is of some interest.

In chart 8.1 the BOP diffusion curve follows the S-shape most clearly. If more detailed data were available, the diffusion curve for FG would also give a similar S-shaped line. For the three technologies that are still far from any degree of saturation, SL, CC and NC, the beginning of an S-shape is also obvious: a slow beginning and then an upturn into the growth phase.

Chart 8.2 shows the pooled data and supports the impression conveyed by the diffusion curves of individual countries concerning the validity of the S-shape but also its irregularity. The slopes are different for each technology, the turning point into growth also differs and therefore the use of an S-curve assumption for various purposes, for example, forecasting, requires caution. Each of the varying S-curves is the result of certain parameters; if the parameters can be correctly assessed and this, precisely, is

Table 8.3. *Selected diffusion indicators*

		Germany	UK	France	Italy	Sweden	US	Japan
Time-lag of introduction (years after pioneer)								
BOP		5	8	4	12	4	8	2
CC		2	8	8	6	11	10	6
SL		1	4	0	6	3	. .	. .
TK		11	*a*	1	3	0	. .	. .
FG		8	0	8	7	18	5	8
NCMT		7	0	2	5	3	0	. .
Time to produce indicated percentage of output, years								
BOP	20	8	5	12	2	9	5	7
	50	13	15	17	. .	13	11	10
CC	10	16	16	14	. .	. .	8	. .
	20	19	20	17	16	12	18	. .
SL^b	10		17	21	. .	. .	. .	. .
	20		21	24	. .	. .	. .	. .
TK^c	10	2	0	12	10	8	. .	. .
	50	21	28	20	19	. .	. .	. .
FG		. .	. .	. .	. .	. .	. .	. .
NCMT^d	1	15	20	21	18	17	19	. .
	(10)	(1977)	(1978)	(. .)	(1974–5)	(1972)	(late 60s)	(1971)
1981^e diffusion (per cent)								
BOP		80	68	82	49	45	61	75
		(96)^f	(100)	(100)	(100)	(97)	(89)	(100)
CC		54	32	51	51	65	21	71
SL^a		9	22	16	12	35	16	4
TK		90	72	90	90	95	. .	. .
FG		100^g	100^g	100^g	68	100^g	. .	. .
NCMT^d		2.2	2.6	1.9	2.2	3.0	. .	. .
		(20)	(18)	(25)	(24)	(35)	(34)	(50)

Source: Chapters 2 to 7 and Nabseth and Ray, *op.cit.*
^{a}UK 1902 omitted as extreme.
^{b}SL share in loom *stock*, based on international statistics.
^{c}Excluding flettons in the UK.
^{d}The ' 1 per cent' data concern stock, the bracketed figures indicate the year when 10 per cent of output was reached (first year of production unknown); diffusion figures concern stocks and production.
^{e}With the following exceptions: TK – 1980; NCMT stock – Germany and Sweden 1980, UK 1982; production – US and Japan 1980.
^{f}Figures in brackets are for BOP + electric steel.
^{g}All flat glass except cast-pressed types.

the usual difficulty, then of course the S-curve can also be estimated with a fair claim to accuracy.

There are some further points arising from the analysis of the data. First, there is the time lag in the adoption of the innovation. This was analysed in more detail elsewhere (Nabseth and Ray, *op.cit*) and it will suffice here to point out that, based on the experiences of the countries included in table 8.3, *on average* it took four to five years before companies in countries other

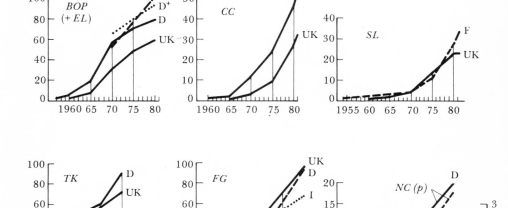

Sources: Chapters 2 to 7.
Notes: Country codes: D – Germany, F – France, I – Italy.
BOP: share in total crude steel production; the lines marked by ' + ' indicate the shares of BOP + Electric steel.
CC: continuously cast steel in total crude steel production.
SL: shuttleless looms in the total stock of looms (national statistics).
TK: bricks burnt in tunnel kilns in total output (in UK excluding flettons).
FG: float in total flat glass output (95 per cent means practically total diffusion).
NC(s): NCMTs in total machine tool stock.
NC(p): NCMTs in total machine tool production.

Chart 8.1 *Diffusion curves, percentages*
(Note changing scales)

than that of the pioneer followed the first commercial application of such innovations as SL or NCMT, novel technologies of major importance requiring relatively modest investment capital. For those representing heavier investment, BOP, CC, TK and FG, this time lag was longer, six to eight years.

Similarly, it takes a long time for a major innovation to spread through industry. In the case of BOP, the only one among the technologies studied that has nearly reached total diffusion (if the other modern method, electric steel, is also taken into account), it took twenty years to approach saturation. But in the cases of CC and TK the same time span was needed to reach only 50 per cent diffusion. The cheaper technologies required even

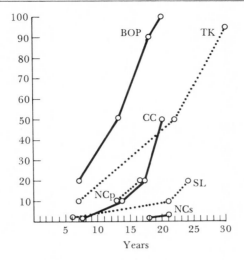

Source: Table 8.4 (see notes to table)

Chart 8.2 *Time-lags in diffusion, diffusion per cent*

more time for a weaker penetration into their respective markets. This is because, among other things, their adoption is not a question of survival to the same extent as in the case of major, revolutionary, new techniques requiring much bigger capital commitment. The risk of non-adoption is correspondingly lower (although this is a rule allowing many possible exceptions).

Apart from information on the timing of diffusion, the findings summed up in the preceding two paragraphs point to one important aspect of the innovation, namely the divisibility or otherwise of the investment incorporating it. To introduce BOP (or CC, TK and FG) usually means the building of a major new plant. This is a piece of equipment of large capacity and the decision to erect it is a very major one on the part of the investor. Once on stream, it produces in large quantities. Hence it is not surprising that the time lag for innovating (that is, following the pioneer) is long; but when built, the new plant immediately takes over significant quantities from the earlier technology and the spread of diffusion is then relatively swift.

By contrast, SLs and NCMTs are smaller pieces of equipment that can be operated, even on a pilot basis, for trials within the existing plant next to the old machines. They may cost more than the traditional machines they replace but the total sum required for their purchase is very modest compared with, say, an oxygen converter, a new kiln or a float line. A

Table 8.4 *Time-lags in innovation and diffusion, years*

	BOP	CC	TK	SL	FG	NCp	NCs
First introduction: average number of years after pioneer							
	6	$7\frac{1}{2}$	6	4	8	..	5
Time to reach degree (per cent) of diffusion[a]							
1	..	$7\frac{1}{2}$	..	..	c	..	18
2	..	..	..	6	..	..	21
10	..	$13\frac{1}{2}$	7	19	..	13	..
20	7	17	..	23	..	17	..
50	13	20	22	..	..	..	..
90	18[b]	..	30	..	..	..	..
100	20[b]	..	..	..	..	..	..

Source: Estimates based on chapters 2 to 7, note 1 and table 8.3.
[a]As measured by output (BOP, CC, TK, NCp) or stock (SL, NCs).
[b]BOP + Electric.
[c]Not applicable.

modern weavery may operate many dozens or several hundreds of looms but it can replace its old looms by SL piecemeal and the same is true in the case of NCMTs. Hence it is easier to decide on their acquisition and there is a shorter introductory time lag, but the very fact that they are divisible may mean their dissemination takes longer. Even progressive companies introduce divisible innovations piecemeal (for very good reasons, such as smoothing out teething troubles and better adaption to local conditions) whereas for large, indivisible systems (for example, BOP, FG, TK) in the case of many plants the decision to introduce or reject a new method of production means all or nothing. Another point is that these large indivisible new systems produce fairly standardised and uniform products, in these instances crude steel, flat glass or bricks, whereas SLs or NCMTs are much more flexible and often used to extend the product mix in areas where the direct costs of production are a relatively smaller proportion of total costs than in the case of the bulk basic materials. This is because the latter are manufactured by the large systems that do not require many of the additional costs like marketing and design that are carried by engineering or textile products.

Using the data in table 8.3 it is possible to obtain an impression of the innovative attitude of the industries of the European countries covered. Any such finding may be misinterpreted, therefore it seems necessary to point to some qualifications that should be borne in mind. First, this is not an Olympic race where performances can be measured accurately and there is nothing else to take account of other than the achievement of the winner. The early adoption and wide diffusion of a major innovation is important from the point of view of competitive success but that is only one, albeit significant, among the many factors that add up to success or failure and there are examples of technological progress and commercial success not necessarily going hand-in-hand. For example, the British steel industry was among the first to abandon the old open hearth method but the fact that all its crude steel production came from up-to-date equipment did not save it from serious troubles, which probably went deeper than those of many other countries. Nor did tunnel kilns save some brick companies from ceasing production.

Secondly, judgement on the basis of the six technologies studied here is naturally limited to these technologies; the inclusion of another six technologies might alter the picture. Thirdly, any such assessment will remain arbitrary and other quantifications may yield different results. Thus these findings should be treated with caution. Nevertheless, the impression conveyed by the data may be summed up briefly as follows.

Among the five European countries, France and the United Kingdom were quickest to adopt these innovations, followed by Germany, Sweden and Italy with about the same time lag after the pioneer. This, however, only relates to the introduction of the innovation in these countries by at least one company. More meaningful, therefore, is the speed of diffusion, that is, the large-scale adoption of the new technique by a significant part of the countries' industry. Taking into account all the diffusion indicators that could be collected on the six technologies, the fastest diffusion was achieved by Sweden, well ahead of the others. Next in line were Germany and Italy. France and the United Kingdom followed with a considerable lag. The two countries which led in the introduction of the six technologies were slowest to disseminate them throughout their industries.

This seems to support one of the statements in the original report which said: 'The analysis of the pooled data suggested a fairly marked negative relationship between the speed of diffusion and the time lag in introduction: in countries which are pioneers, diffusion tends to be *slower*. This result is consistent with the hypothesis that the pioneer faces all sorts of teething troubles – new problems associated with the new technique – which are likely to be solved, partly and gradually, by the time others adopt it. It is therefore not necessarily desirable to be the first to introduce a new technique' (Nabseth and Ray, *op.cit.* p.19).

Again, this suggestion must be treated with caution. Special circumstances influence the adoption of new techniques and there are exceptions to the soft rule suggested above indicating that there might be cases showing the opposite: that the pioneer achieves the most rapid diffusion. Float glass in the United Kingdom is a case in point.

By 1981 Sweden again leads the other European countries in terms of the diffusion of the six technologies. No marked difference becomes apparent between the other countries without weighting the industries affected, though the United Kingdom does seem to lag behind.

The technologies studied were relatively new in the 1960s. Their fundamental principles did not change during the 1970s or early 1980s but each of them has been further developed; the extent of the development has been different, but the directions were the same: widening the scope of the new methods and raising their efficiency and reliability.

The steel processes, BOP and CC, have been extended into other types of steel, shuttleless looms have been modified to make more colourful and wider fabrics, and the float process has been adapted to make thinner glass. The development in these cases has been gradual. The installation of a computer on the NC machine tools themselves was a more important change but it had the same result of greatly enlarging the scope of this technology.

This general improvement in new technologies which have already been applied commercially raises a number of points. Each of these six technologies was originally devised to carry out certain specific jobs, for example, BOP was meant to produce bulk steel, CC was first applied to special steels and the float process was to make polished plate glass. Having successfully fulfilled the original purpose, the next step was to extend their scope; in the case of the float process to make window glass, for example. The extension required considerable research and development but its eventual success added significantly to the usefulness of the new technology. Bearing this in mind, one could argue that in many cases diffusion is never complete: the technology can be developed further and applied to new areas of production.[5]

Even within the relatively narrow scope of our study there are examples of this. Thus, given more detailed information, the diffusion curves of SL and NC could be further subdivided into a series of consecutive, shorter S-curves representing the various, more and more sophisticated, types of SLs and NCs. (This is particularly noticeable with regard to the conversion of NC into CNC, or the subsequent generation of SLs.) Each of the sub-curves represents some advance.

In each of the cases studied there is scope for further development. In a number of cases the direction of development is fairly clear and it seems to be only a question of time before the new objective is realised: in other cases the future is less clear and only minor adjustments can be foreseen with our present knowledge. If, however, the history of these six technologies can be taken as any sort of guide, further advance appears very probable, although neither its extent nor its timing can be guaranteed or precisely foreseen.

It follows that any technological ceiling can be considered only in a dynamic context: a new technology may be limited by a technological ceiling today but in a few years' time the same limitation may be largely or entirely removed by the improvement of the technology. A good deal of the diffusion process of these technologies consisted of widening the applicability of the original innovation, extending it into new areas by means of step-by-step development. Most of this technical advance was not exogenous to industry: it was endogenously generated by the development efforts of the suppliers of the equipment, who often relied on the experiences and suggestions regarding the requirements of the users of the technology. Competition among suppliers provides a great stimulus in the direction of technical progress, such as in the case of shuttleless looms. In a few other cases, the users of the technology developed it further themselves.

DECLINE OF THE OLD TECHNOLOGY

The new technology gradually replaces the old, but the timing of the replacement and the degree of penetration of the new technique varies a great deal, depending on the nature of the technology, on the economic conditions, such as the stage of development of the country and the economic cycle, as well as on the operators of the technology, the companies that eventually decide on adopting or rejecting the new.

The six technologies studied are of different natures and importance. The two steel technologies, BOP and CC, as well as float glass, are of revolutionary significance in the manufacture of steel or glass. They have changed the respective manufacturing processes entirely. The tunnel kiln was a great step forward in brickmaking but not as radical as these three innovations. Because of the indivisible nature of these four technologies their diffusion has occurred in a different manner from the two divisible ones, namely SL and NCMT. Divisibility has meant a better chance for survival of the older techniques, at least for a time.

Some of the technologies included in this study provide the basis for a theoretical observation concerning the rise and decline of major processes. Starting from zero a new technology grows at first slowly but later speeds up and once more slows down as its penetration approaches 100 per cent or some lower ceiling figure. This is the familiar S-shape. However, after staying at the top for a period it falls off again back towards zero as it is supplanted by the next wave of technology. It is replaced by an even newer process and the length of the period whilst the first technology can remain at the peak depends on the emergence of the second.

The disadvantage of the S-shaped curve (or the logistic curve, as a good representation of the S-curve) is that once the technology has reached its peak it appears to stay there for ever. What chart 2.1 suggests (page 6) on the steel technologies is that an equally good, indeed better, representation is that the *whole* wave of the technology, from birth through maximum use to death, might follow the bell shape of a normal distribution curve, although the right-hand side of the curve may fall more steeply. Vastly improved information and communication must have contributed to the fact that the decline of the open hearth method of steelmaking was much faster than the decline of the Bessemer method, the previous dominant steelmaking process. Its slowing down towards the end of the decline and its final elimination will probably also be quicker. The study of float glass conveys the same message: it has replaced the earlier processes of making flat glass within a relatively short time; the previous technology stayed at its peak for a long time but its fall has been precipitous.

The environment in the advanced industrial countries differs from that in the developing areas and to some extent from those in centrally planned economies. It has been said that, 'technical change is a cumulative process specific to firms: what they can realistically try to do technically in the future is strongly conditioned by what they have been able to do in the past'.[5] Another interpretation of the same idea is that the newest, most sophisticated technologies have little chance of succeeding and hence probably would not be tried unless they can be built upon a general technical background that is already fairly advanced. Very great technical jumps are unlikely to lead to success and there are many reasons for rejecting them, at least temporarily, because neither can the level of training and education of the operating personnel provide the hope, let alone the guarantee, that the sophisticated equipment will work, nor are the supporting external services available to maintain its proper operation. There are also cases in many LDCs where the installation of the most advanced equipment is not justified on the grounds of reducing costs or saving labour and the latter objective may not even be desired. Many centrally planned economies protect their industries in various ways, shielding them from competition from the products of more advanced technologies. Thus, when comparing the diffusion of these and other new technologies in the advanced and relatively open economies with that of the other countries, crudely categorised as developing and/or centrally planning, some fundamental differences have to be borne in mind.

Analysis of the findings presented in chapters 2 to 7 indicates that these six technologies leave no easily definable room for the survival of the older methods of production. In many of the advanced countries the old steelmaking technologies have been abandoned already. BOP and electric steel account for the whole of steel output and it is just a question of time before the earlier technologies disappear entirely from the steelworks. The centrally planned economies are, however, still employing the open hearth process to a large extent and it seems that this older technology will survive, albeit with declining significance, for some time to come. In many less developed countries the question does not arise since their steel production (mostly in mini-mills) is based on electric furnaces; where open hearth techniques do exist, their conversion will also take longer.

Continuous casting still has a long way to go to reach universal application, even in the advanced countries. It will be developed further but the conventional casting system is likely to be retained for particular types of commercial steel and for special products. The tunnel kiln requires more complicated equipment than the earlier kiln types and also assumes a relatively high volume of production; nevertheless, the earlier technology will remain in operation for products made in small quantities or for very small local works; furthermore, given the long life of a kiln, old kilns may survive for a time once written off and carrying no capital cost at all. This is also the case in the example of earlier technology fighting back with some limited success by the development of a modified kiln which operates on the earlier principle, albeit applying to it so many improvements and alterations that the whole almost adds up to a new type of kiln.

In the manufacture of flat glass the float process has been a winner except in the making of pressed/cast glass or very thin glass. But the capacity of a float line is too large for a small market: the earlier techniques continue to survive in a small country with high *per capita* glass demand, or a larger country with low demand.

Shuttleless looms are on the way to replacing the bulk of conventional shuttle looms in the advanced countries, and to some extent in the less developed countries too. They can do most of the work of shuttle looms, but not all (as yet). For these small 'pockets' the old looms are still being used. The replacement of the large stock of traditional looms will take a long time even in the advanced countries. Elsewhere, for example, in Asia with one half of the world's looms, SLs may spread slowly but may never wholly replace the traditional looms because cheap and abundant labour reduces the incentive to change and the environmental protection of workers (from noise) is also considered less important at present.

Numerical control, after the developments in microelectronics, has been on the rise for some time. Its application to metalworking machine tools has been spreading but NCMTs still account for no more than a tiny percentage of the national machine tool park. Conventional machines and automatic ones, catering for high volume production, have not been made redundant by the NC technique. Automatics will probably survive, whilst the gradual replacement of the former by NCMTs is unlikely to become total. Many of the conventional machines, of sophisticated varieties but without NC, will be retained for special work or the machining of small

numbers. The spreading of robots may also influence the future application of NCMTs.

Thus, in almost every case there are small areas in the advanced
countries, and much vaster ones elsewhere, that are unlikely to be taken
over by the new technology, at least given the present state of knowledge.
Much depends, however, on the further development of these technologies.
In almost every case the original technology has already been further
developed and changed in order to extend its applicability and efficiency
(in both technical and economic senses). The previous chapters provide
plenty of evidence of this. It is conceivable, therefore, that this process will
continue and reduce the possibilities for the survival of the conventional
methods.

SIZE

Our investigations indicate that size has less to do with the diffusion of new
technologies in the mature phase than was believed some ten or twenty
years ago. It is not denied that large companies have certain advantages (as
have countries with large industries) in terms of the access to investment
capital, the availability of particular skills and, often though certainly not
always, the general technical level onto which it is easier to graft anything
of higher sophistication. Nevertheless, there are plenty of examples of
medium-sized or smaller companies pioneering. However, after the initial
phases of the innovation, once the new technology has matured and is
receiving growing acceptance, company size appears gradually to lose its
significance.

The divisible technologies, in our case SLs and NCMTs, can be applied
on a small scale. Certain economies of scale are naturally achieved if the
new looms or machine tools are installed in some number constituting a
group that can be looked after by the same number of workers that would
be needed to operate or maintain just one or two of them. The other
technologies which we classified crudely as indivisible present some
limitations: their capacity assumes a minimum output threshold that may
be too high for a smaller producer. In steelmaking the solution is simple:
instead of BOP, the electric furnace is the answer. But a small tunnel kiln is
uneconomical for bricks and a float line produces quantities of glass that
are too large for certain markets.

Apart from the size of the market, of the company or the plant, size can
be interpreted at a more micro level: that of the quantity produced or the
batch size. In the case of NCMTs, for example, this has significant
implications on the diffusion of the NC technique that is particularly suited
to batch sizes within certain limits or having specific characteristics.

These technologies were already on the upswing before the energy prices started to rise dramatically in 1973–4. BOP, CC, FG and TK are energy savers, as compared with the technologies they replace; it is therefore likely that their diffusion might have been accelerated by the higher energy prices. Since the diffusion of these processes was already in the growth phase by 1973 it is not possible to quantify the effect of the higher energy prices. It is almost certain, however, that CC was helped most by the increasing energy costs.

The energy price effect on SL and NCMT is less clear. In both cases the innovation yields less energy saving and the importance of energy in total production costs is also less than in the four cases above. Nevertheless, at least in the case of NCMTs, the reference to higher energy prices and to the advantages offered by the new machine having a beneficial indirect effect on energy cost, has been used to justify the investment. Changes in the relative prices of the various fuels may have considerable influence on their use in those processes that admit alternative fuels. It is, for example, conceivable that the relative cost advantage of coal in recent years, if it lasts, will make the burning of gas less exclusive in tunnel kilns and improved methods will be developed to promote the use of coal in them, reducing or eliminating its disadvantages.

THE ROLE OF THE STATE

In the course of this investigation we have found several forms of state intervention. This may take the form of direct measures with a particular objective or a blanket type general approach. The more direct measures were specific schemes aimed at promoting a particular innovation (such as the British scheme for NCMTs) or some major action to subsidise or otherwise save some sector of industry (in our case, the cotton or steel industry) of a particular country. These were exceptional however. Special 'soft loans' to industry, to assist investment and reconstruction, already have a wider relevance. A much more generally valid case was made by the companies we approached in the course of this work and also by the institutes associated with this project, in favour of leaving industry alone but creating an economic climate favourable to investment, with the promise of sustainable economic growth. This is obviously more difficult than any of the direct measures.

NOTES

NOTE TO CHAPTER 1

1 L. Nabseth and G.F. Ray (eds), *The diffusion of new industrial processes*, Cambridge University Press, 1974.

NOTES TO CHAPTER 2

1 J.R. Meyer and G. Herregat, 'The basic oxygen steel process', Chapter 6 in Nabseth and Ray, *op. cit.*
2 G. Rosegger, 'Exploratory evaluations of major technological innovations: basic oxygen furnaces and continuous casting', Part II in B. Gold, G. Rosegger and M.G. Boylan, Jr., *Evaluating Technological Innovations*, Lexington, Mass., D.C. Heath & Co., 1980.
3 A perfect definition of the mini-mill is still lacking. A UN/ECE study (1979) attempted to define it as follows: 'A mini-mill operates one or several electric arc furnaces followed either by continuous casting or roughing rolling mill and finishing mill; its size is up to 500,000 tonnes a year; its programme of production is relatively simple and it is basically serving local demand'. Other sources define it differently. In the mini-mill report of the Metal Bulletin (*Mini-mill monographs*, a supplement to *Metal Bulletin Monthly*, December 1981) firms with capacities from 70,000 tonnes to over one million tonnes are listed and it is clearly stated: 'no two mini-mills are the same'.
4 To name some: OLP – oxygen + lime powder; LD/CB – combination blowing; Q-BOP – bottom blowing; COIN – coal-oxygen injection; OBM – oxygen-bottom-Maxhütte; AOD (in stainless steel production) – argon-oxygen decarburisation.
5 This finding is similar to that of B. Carlsson who documented the growing size of integrated steel *enterprises* in, B. Carlsson, 'Structure and performance in the West European steel industry: a historical perspective', in H.W. de Jong, (ed) *The Structure of European Industry*, Amsterdam, M. Nijhoff, 1981.
6 See O.J.W. Gilbert, 'Innovation in the steel industry – the vice of scale', *The Royal Society of Arts Journal*, August 1981, p.577.
7 See the *Metal Bulletin Monthly*, July 1982, p.61.

NOTES TO CHAPTER 3

1 See W. Schenk, 'Continuous casting of steel', chapter 9 in Nabseth and Ray, *op.cit.*

2 *Metal Bulletin Monthly*, no. 140, August 1982 (special report on CC).
3 H. Spitzer and K.J. Kremer, 'Die Entwicklung metallurgischer Verfahren und ihre Auswirkung auf die Eigenschaften von Qualitäts- und Edelstahlen', *VDI Berichte* Nr 428, 1981.
4 Das Giessrad steigert die Stahlgussleistung. *Blick durch die Wirtschaft*, 22 March 1983.

NOTES TO CHAPTER 4

1 L.A. Lacci, S.W. Davies and R.J. Smith, 'Tunnel kilns in brickmaking', chapter 5 in Nabseth and Ray, *op.cit.*
2 J.T.S. Corbett, 'Energy conservation kiln developments: efficient energy usage in a suspended roof continuous kiln', presented to The British Ceramic Society, April 1978.
3 Among others, H. Lingl, Die Energiekrise bestimmt die Entwicklung der Ziegelindustrie während der achtziger Jahre, *Keramische Zeitschrift*, No. 11, 1980; B. Gottschalk, Die Verwendung von Kohle in der keramischen Industrie, Keramische Zeitschrift, No. 11, 1980; Verbesserung am Tunnelofenbetrieb, besonders im Hinblick auf Einsparung von Brennstoffen, *Keramische Zeitschrift*, No. 1, 1981; G. Werkmeister, Wärmewirtschaftliche Verbesserungen beim Betrieb keramischer Tunnelöfen, *Keramische Zeitschrift* No. 7, 1981; and so on.
4 Brick Capacity Survey, *Housing construction statistics*, Department of the Environment, 1976.
5 *Bricks and Tiles*, Keynote Publications, 1979.

NOTES TO CHAPTER 5

1 See R.J. Smith, 'Shuttleless looms', chapter 10 in Nabseth and Ray, *op.cit.*
2 R. Rothwell, 'Innovation in textile machinery', in K. Pavitt (ed), *Technical innovation and British economic performance*, London, Macmillan, 1980.
3 The European Community textile industry, *European file* (issued by the EC), 7/82, April 1982.
4 The statistics on automatic looms and on total looms are in some respects not strictly comparable.
5 The definitions of the national statistics differ somewhat from those of the international statistics presented in other parts of this chapter.
6 C.M. Miles, *Lancashire textiles: a case study in industrial change*, NIESR Occasional paper no 23, Cambridge University Press, 1968.
7 A. Chadwick, 'The changing pattern of the world weaving industry', *Textile Month*, September 1978.
8 R. Leutert, Wohin geht die Entwicklung im Webmaschinenbau, (Trends in weaving machine design) *Melliand Textilberichte*, 2/1981.

NOTES TO CHAPTER 6

1 See Nabseth and Ray, *op.cit.* chapter 7, p.204.
2 Flachglasindustrie: Kampf um Positionen, *Wirtschaftswoche* Nr 48, 26 November 1982.

NOTES TO CHAPTER 7

1 A. Gebhardt and O. Hatzold, 'Numerically controlled machine tools', chapter
   3 in Nabseth and Ray, *op.cit.*
2 *Wirtschaftliche und soziale Auswirkungen des CNC-Werkzeugmaschineneinsatzes,*
   Fraunhofer-Institut, 1981 (RKW project A 133, Bestell Nr 758).
3 A. Bollard, 'Technology, economic change and small firms', *Lloyds Bank Review,*
   no. 147, January 1983 and *Tooling up or tooling down,* Intermediate Technology
   Development Group, 1982 (mimeo).
4 Because of possible small differences in definition the various countries' figures
   may not be strictly comparable.
5 The Shorter Oxford English Dictionary (1968) defines a robot as 'a machine
   devised to function in place of a living agent, one which acts automatically or
   with a minimum of external impulse'. The later (1979) edition of the American
   Webster's New Collegiate Dictionary agrees with this but goes further: a robot
   'performs complex acts; [it is] an automatic apparatus or device that performs
   functions ordinarily ascribed to human beings or operates with what appears to
   be almost human intelligence'.

NOTES TO CHAPTER 8

1 Nabseth and Ray, *op.cit.*
2 W.E.G. Salter, *Productivity and Technical Change,* Cambridge University Press,
   1960. Salter's best practice is the most up-to-date technique at each date, having
   regard to both economic and technical conditions and yielding minimum costs
   in terms of the production function and relative factor prices. Graphically
   represented, plants with best practice technique constitute the head of the
   diagram whilst other plants, in declining order of efficiency, constitute the tail
   with the least efficient ones at the end of the tail.
3 *VDW Bericht 1/80*: Altersstruktur des industriellen Werkzeugmaschinenparks in
   der BRD, Frankfurt, December 1980.
4 S. Davies, *The diffusion of process innovations,* Cambridge University Press, 1979.
5 The findings in this section are relevant to the theorising and modelbuilding
   about innovation diffusion in recent literature and justify empirically the points
   made by Gold and Metcalfe, amongst others, about the importance of technical
   change during the diffusion process. See B. Gold, Technological diffusion in
   industry: research needs and shortcomings, *Journal of Industrial Economics,* March
   1981; J.S. Metcalfe, Impulse and diffusion in the study of technical change,
   Futures 13, no. 5.
6 K. Pavitt, *Patterns of technical change: evidence, theory and policy implications,* Imperial
   College 'Science and Technology' lecture, March 1983 (mimeo).

INDEX

RECENT PUBLICATIONS OF THE
NATIONAL INSTITUTE OF ECONOMIC
AND SOCIAL RESEARCH

published by
THE CAMBRIDGE UNIVERSITY PRESS

THE NATIONAL INSTITUTE OF ECONOMIC AND
SOCIAL RESEARCH

publishes regularly

THE NATIONAL INSTITUTE ECONOMIC REVIEW

A quarterly analysis of the general economic situation in the United Kingdom and the world overseas, with forecasts eighteen months ahead. The last issue each year contains an assessment of medium-term prospects. There are also in most issues special articles on subjects of interest to academic and business economists.

Annual subscriptions, £30.00 (home), and £40.00 (abroad), also single issues for the current year, £8.50 (home) and £12.00 (abroad), are available directly from NIESR, 2 Dean Trench Street, Smith Square, London, SW1P 3HE.

Subscriptions at the special reduced price of £12.00 p.a. are available to students in the United Kingdom and Irish Republic on application to the Secretary of the Institute.

Back numbers and reprints of issues which have gone out of stock are distributed by Wm. Dawson and Sons Ltd., Cannon House, Park Farm Road, Folkestone. Microfiche copies for the years 1959–82 are available from EP Microform Ltd, Bradford Road, East Ardsley, Wakefield, Yorks.

Published by
HEINEMANN EDUCATIONAL BOOKS
THE UNITED KINGDOM ECONOMY
by the NIESR. 5th edn, 1982. pp.119. £1.95 net.
DEMAND MANAGEMENT
Edited by MICHAEL POSNER. 1978. pp.256. £6.50 (paperback) net.
DE-INDUSTRIALISATION
Edited by FRANK BLACKABY. 1979. pp.282. £9.50 (hardback), £6.50 (paperback) net.
BRITAIN'S TRADE AND EXCHANGE-RATE POLICY
Edited by ROBIN MAJOR. 1979. pp.240. £14.50 (hardback), £6.50 (paperback) net.
BRITAIN IN EUROPE
Edited by WILLIAM WALLACE. 1980. pp.224. £14.50 (hardback), £6.50 (paperback) net.
THE FUTURE OF PAY BARGAINING
Edited by FRANK BLACKABY. 1980. pp.246. £14.50 (hardback), £6.50 (paperback) net.
INDUSTRIAL POLICY AND INNOVATION
Edited by CHARLES CARTER. 1981. pp.241. £14.50 (hardback), £6.50 (paperback) net.
THE CONSTITUTION OF NORTHERN IRELAND
Edited by DAVID WATT. 1981. pp.227. £15.00 (hardback), £7.50 (paperback) net.
RETIREMENT POLICY THE NEXT FIFTY YEARS
Edited by MICHAEL FOGARTY. 1982. pp.216. £14.00 (hardback), £6.50 (paperback) net.
SLOWER GROWTH IN THE WESTERN WORLD
Edited by R.C.O. MATTHEWS. 1982. pp.176. £14.50 (hardback), £6.50 (paperback) net.
NATIONAL INTERESTS AND LOCAL GOVERNMENT
Edited by KEN YOUNG. 1983. pp.172. £15.00 (hardback), £7.50 (paperback) net.
EMPLOYMENT, OUTPUT AND INFLATION
Edited by A.J.C. BRITTON. 1983. pp.196. £19.50 net.
THE TROUBLED ALLIANCE. THE US AND WESTERN EUROPE IN THE 1980s
Edited by Professor LAWRENCE FREEDMAN. 1983. p.176. £16.50 (hardback), £6.50 (paperback) net.